THE RISING SOUTH

Volume 1
Changes and Issues

The Rising South

Volume 1

Changes and Issues

EDITED BY

Donald R. Noble and Joab L. Thomas

THE UNIVERSITY OF ALABAMA PRESS
University, Alabama

Library of Congress Cataloging in Publication Data

The Rising South

  Includes index.
  CONTENTS: v. 1. Changes and issues.
1. Southern States—Politics and government—1951-
—Addresses, essays, lectures. 2. Southern states—
Economic conditions—1945- —Addresses, essays,
lectures. 3. Southern States—Civilization—Addresses,
essays, lectures. I. Noble, Donald R. II. Thomas,
Joab L.
F216.2.R57   975'.04   75-22254
ISBN 0-8173-5316-X

Contents

Acknowledgments

The editors wish to thank The University of Alabama and the Interim Term in particular for providing funds for the administration of this symposium. We also wish to thank Martha Rogers and Virginia Dodson for their numerous contributions to the administration of the symposium and the editing of the manuscript, and for their cheerfulness throughout.

THE RISING SOUTH

Volume 1
Changes and Issues

Introduction

DONALD R. NOBLE

George B. Tindall wryly begins the keynote address of the symposium from which most of these papers are taken with a quote from Ecclesiastes, "there is no new thing under the sun," and the comment that the symposium on the "New" or the "changing" or, indeed, the "rising" South is "one of the flourishing minor industries of the region." He goes on to enumerate a few of the events and books that have been dedicated to this subject, going back to 1892 when the *Review of Reviews* ran an article about a recent symposium held to discuss the "New South."

True, the South has been a region greatly given to self-examination and self-consciousness, as he asserts, but not without good reason, for it is in this region, with its strong belief in, even reverence for, tradition, family, the past, that great changes have come and come most abruptly. The South has at various times been solid, silent, sullen, but in spite of what appears from the outside to be a desire to stay the same, to lie back in the sultry heat and practice the American version of *dolce farniente*, it has not been possible. This region, not the change-oriented, presumably fast-paced, future-shocked Northeast, has been the scene of Civil War, emancipation, the Reconstruction regime, the "New South." And in the twentieth century, as Tindall reminds us, "we have watched the landmarks topple in rapid succession: the one-crop agriculture, the one-crop industry, the one-party system, the white primary, the poll tax, racial segregation—indeed so many foundations of the old order [have crumbled] that we now live in a post-New South which nobody has yet given a name."

Perhaps it is just this, a desire to understand our post-New

1

South, that is the motivation for our frequent spates of self-study. This region has switched to and from cotton, into and out of the soil bank and is now planting soybeans; this region has known defeat, alienation, and reconstruction; this region, which has been held in contempt by many Americans for its racial practices, now watches, on television, the integration of the Boston school system; this region, the most homogeneous in the nation, reads in the paper that not only is Northern industry moving South, as usual, but that Japanese investors are buying up large chunks of what we have always thought of as Scarlet O'Hara's Atlanta.

All of this should come as no surprise, since it has been going on now for a hundred and fifty years. Indeed, C. Vann Woodward, in his *The Strange Career of Jim Crow*, has told us that Southerners should be "the last Americans to expect indefinite continuity of their institutions and social arrangements." But having it said does not seem to help all that much, and the question "what is going on now?" brings forth, in very American style, the symposium.

The subjects of these symposia have traditionally been politics, race, and economics. But to these standards we, in the post-New South, must add at least three new ones: education, the arts, and the environment. In many cases the old concerns, the old needs, come into conflict with the new concerns, the new needs. That is the case in the first pair of papers in this collection.

Barney Weeks, president of the Alabama Labor Council, AFL-CIO, has devoted his life to the union movement and to the betterment of working conditions in the mines and factories of Alabama. His paper is a proud résumé of accomplishments in the labor field: employment is up; per capita income is up; the number of new industries in Alabama increases every day.

These new jobs mean new paychecks, of course, and new industry has traditionally been the goal of the labor movement in Alabama as it has been the goal of state and local agencies throughout the South. Now, Weeks insists, we must raise our sights. Workers in Alabama earn less than workers in other states because Alabama, like other Southern states, has traditionally taken what industry she could get, and what she could get was often low-paying, socially irresponsible textile mills that took advantage of the surplus of unskilled labor or industries that located near the sources of raw materials, took those raw materials, and moved on. From here on, Weeks argues, we must be more selective. Progress has been made, but more progress can be made with industries such as the General Motors plant going up in Limestone County or the chemical works being constructed in Mobile.

One can only agree with this argument, but with reservations. Verda Horne, a dedicated environmentalist, counsels caution. Let us have the petroleum plants, chemical plants, paper mills, she says, but let us insist, in advance, that these industries be environmentally responsible. Let us be sure we have not lost more in natural beauty and resources than we have gained in paychecks. If the land is stripped, the air and water fouled forever, our new high-paying industries will have been a very mixed blessing indeed.

By way of underscoring this warning and to illustrate what the land here was once like and what we have already done to it, Horne writes of the experiences of four early visitors to Alabama: William Bartram, the botanist, Hugo De Vries, the Dutch pioneer in plant mutations, Sir Charles Lyell, the English geologist, and Philip Gosse, an Englishman who came to teach in a small private school near Selma. These men saw an Alabama that is in part gone, and in larger part threatened. They observed and wrote about the Carolina parakeet, now extinct, and the strata of the cliffs along the Alabama River, a rich source of information for historical geologists. They wrote about interesting native wildflowers—the giant primrose—a rare species related to the plants that De Vries worked with in developing his mutation theory of evolution. These rare plants still survive, but in small and threatened numbers. We need the industries of the future, but we also need to preserve the flora and the fauna that Horne describes so movingly.

Tom Gilmore, the first black sheriff of Greene County, Alabama, like Verda Horne, is sensitive to the natural beauty of his homeland and, like Barney Weeks, knows the great importance of developing new industries and creating new jobs in order to improve the living conditions in his county, one of the poorest in the nation. He works actively and with some success in attracting new industry to Greene County. Sheriff Gilmore's first objective, however, has been to give the people of Greene County what he feels they have not ever had and what they must have, even before larger paychecks—he means to see that all the citizens of Greene County have justice under the law.

Tom Gilmore speaks with pride of his experiences with Dr. Martin Luther King, Jr., and the S.C.L.C. He relates the story of his growing involvement in the civil rights movement of the 1960's —the boycotts, marches, and demonstrations—and the voting rights acts, which led to widespread black voter registration and his own election as sheriff.

Since that election, in which the county offices of Greene County, Alabama, were won by blacks for the first time since Reconstruction, Gilmore has been more than sheriff to the people of Greene County. He serves them as social worker, counselor, and friend and as spokesman to the "outside" world, informing that world of the progress being made in living conditions and human rights in this small section of rural Alabama. Gilmore does not hold up Greene County as a model of perfection, but he proudly insists that it *is* an example of what can be achieved in a democracy, through determination and nonviolence.

In the fifties and sixties Pat Derian also was an active participant in the struggle for equal rights for blacks in the Deep South. More recently, however, she has focused her attention on the achievement of political, legal, and economic equality for women, and Southern women in particular.

Derian begins her essay by outlining the stereotypes with which Southern women are presently burdened. If the lady is white, the myth has it, she is predestined to be a sorority girl, a schoolteacher, a wife, a churchwoman, a mother, and a widow. She will be prudish, Christian, tidy, and probably frigid. If she is black, the story goes, she will be either a beloved Mammy or a sexy, promiscuous and, therefore, dangerous black girl or a strong, castrating matriarch. These myths, though often promoted by Southern women themselves, are counterproductive, even danger-ous, Derian tells us, and obscure the facts about what Southern women are really doing.

What they are doing, black and white women both, is working, because they and/or their families need the money. They are often working at jobs with little status and usually being paid less for their work than men doing the same jobs. Part of the reason for this, Derian argues, is the myth that these Southern females are helpless, inefficient, dependent, and undependable. Southern women are not as active in the movement to achieve equal rights as women in other parts of the nation, partly because so many have been taken in by the stereotypes that purport to represent them, but the tide is changing and more and more women in the South are voicing the same demands: equal pay for equal work, greater political participation, and the passage of the Equal Rights Amendment. The going is tougher for women in the South, Derian says, because they "have had to climb off a rickety pedestal and through an awful lot of heavy syrup," but the going is steady. Southern women are not much different from women in other sections, Derian insists, but they have the advantage, perhaps, of knowing the worst about themselves and perhaps possess fewer illusions. They are also developing an increased awareness of their own economic, moral, and political power.

These many changes in the twentieth-century South—changes in politics, economics, human rights, concern for the environment —while important and obvious, even dramatic to Southerners, have passed largely unnoticed outside the region. Through the thirties and forties especially, the rest of the nation had little knowledge of or interest in what was going on down in Dixie. People in the rest of the country gave the South little thought except for one seemingly inexplicable phenomenon: the Southern Literary Renascence. In the thirties and forties the South produced a prodigious number of gifted writers: not only Faulkner, Wolfe, Caldwell, and Williams, the Nashville writers—Tate, Ransom, Warren—but writers now held in less esteem, such as Kroll or

Caldwell, and the women, Eudora Welty being the best of them.

It was all too good to be true, people said at first. Then, its truth certain, critics insisted it was too good to last; a nova of this magnitude would inevitably be brief. It became for some a kind of literary-critical game, judging whether it was over and, if it were not, how much longer it could last.

The "generation" immediately following the Renascence did not let the home team down. William Styron, Walker Percy, Flannery O'Connor, Carson McCullers, the generation of the fifties, continued the Renascence. The question now is this: is it over now?

By way of answer, Louis D. Rubin, Jr., Professor of English at the University of North Carolina and a leading authority on Southern literature, begs the question because, he insists, the question is meaningless, unimportant. Whether Walter Sullivan of Vanderbilt is right and the Renascence is over or, as Rubin has argued, the Renascence continues, is beside the point. The job of the reader and critic of today is to examine the writers of today, on their own terms, not by comparison with Faulkner or Warren. Why should we expect the work of writers in their twenties and thirties to "be like" the work of writers in their fifties and sixties, especially when the prevailing mode of the last fifty years in the South has been *change?* This new writing, written by Southerners in the South, *is* Southern writing, but it reflects the South of today, not the depression South of 1935, or some other South.

Rubin thus asks that the question "is the Southern Literary Renascence over?" be put to rest and that critics, younger critics especially, expend their energies in more useful ways, that is, in assessing and making available to the contemporary reader the work of our younger writers.

Rubin closes his essay by declaring his own disinclination to do this job. Following the example of Edmund Wilson, Rubin will continue to discuss the work of the writers of *his* generation and examine the work of their forebears. He challenges the younger critics of Southern Literature to take up the task of evaluating the work of *their* generation.

The last two essays in this collection, like George Tindall's contribution, are more general in nature in their discussions of recent changes in the South, and where the region is headed. David Mathews, president of The University of Alabama, is often invited to address himself to these questions, and his essay is in part a running summary of statements he has made over the past few years, capped by his personal report on what the Commission on the Future of the South, an agency of the Southern Growth Policies Board, took to be the most pressing problems facing the South at this time.

Mathews traces the rising hopes and subsequent disillusionments that have accompanied other "New Souths." The industrialized New South of Henry Grady, for example, may have simply traded agricultural poverty for cotton mill poverty. Mathews notes how the South has often measured itself by comparison with the North and how this standard of comparison is, now more than ever, foolish. Why would the South wish to achieve the urban blight, social problems, and ruined natural environments of so many other areas of the country? The South is different from other regions—having known defeat, failure, and poverty in the land of Benjamin Franklin and Horatio Alger, having known guilt in a land so often thought of, by Americans, as innocent, in sharp contrast to the fallen state of older cultures, European and Asian. The South is unlike the rest of America and, in fact, may have more in common with the Old World than with the New.

Thus, the experiences, the sophistication if you will, of the South, coupled with the ironic fact that in its slowness the region has not yet used up its natural resources or spoiled its environment, may, as some think, put the newest New South in a position to lead the rest of the nation, now so confused and dispirited, politically and economically.

The South, "New" as it may be, still possesses traditional beliefs and habits of great value for her now: the willingness to fight for a cause, pride, independence, hospitality, love of the land, and a sense of community and home. These old-fashioned virtues, combined with one more, hope (The South Shall Rise Again), can

serve the region in good stead. Southerners, despite the protesta-
tions of John Egerton to the contrary, are not yet fully "Americanized," and it is probably a good thing for the South and for the
nation.

While David Mathews writes of the potential leadership for
the nation to be found in the South, his essay is essentially regional.
Peter Schrag, on the other hand, is more national in his concerns
and in his viewpoint. A free-lance writer and former editor of
Saturday Review, and no Southerner by any stretch of the imagination, Schrag has covered stories in the South several times over
the past few years and has a perspective worth sharing.

Schrag speaks of the North's "need" for the South as the nation's
last frontier, America's last chance for a new start. He acknowl-
edges that the South still possesses many of the old virtues but
points out that two rather contradictory ideas are simultaneously
current: the South as "Redeemer" and "the South as catching up
with the rest of the nation," as in the aphorism "Southern Progress
without Northern Mistakes."

"Outsiders" are much interested in the South, Schrag notes,
and may expect too much of her. Black candidates can run for
office without being lynched, but unless there is a large black
majority, they usually lose. Northerners, and Northern newsmen
and liberals in particular, Schrag admits somewhat ruefully, have
underestimated the difficulties of integration and the dangers of
being a "liberal" in the South. At one time "liberalism" and
liberal rhetoric could be as dangerous here as they were chic in
Cambridge or Berkeley. Southern activists of the fifties and sixties
deserve even more credit, perhaps, than they have been given.

Things change in the South, Schrag says, but they change slowly and sometimes grudgingly. Many Southerners wish to resist
change, freeze time, but it is not the world of 1850 they wish to
keep forever, it is the world of 1950, a time in which they had
"joined" the rest of the country and were members of the Union
in good standing, but had not yet been expected to live up to the
Brown Decision of 1954 and all the hard issues that followed it.

A New South has come into being since the Second World War,

Schrag agrees, but it is not geographic, is not comprised of the states of the Confederacy. Rather, it is a tier of states south of a line drawn from Richmond to San Jose, a tier of states with much in common: Republicanism, conservatism, dependence on technologies such as air conditioning and irrigation, military bases, oil and defense industry. Liberals now hail from the Midwest, the old "heartland," Schrag reminds us; Nixon pursued a Southern strategy, but it encompassed Arizona as well as Mississippi.

So this continent-wide New South is the real political and economic new South, not the Old Confederacy. Nevertheless, the nation does face new problems, and the Old South may retain some of the answers. In a nation that Schrag sees as increasingly conformist, increasingly intolerant of eccentricity, and given to all manner of bugging and surveillance, Southerners' insistence on privacy and the right of every individual to live as he pleases may serve us well. The South has always lived with its eccentrics and tolerated craziness, Schrag says—the literature of the South is noted for its "grotesques"—the South will continue, he hopes, through men like Senator Sam Ervin, to protect these rights. In the meantime, the region must "develop," but she must at the same time beware of becoming Los Angeles.

Joseph Doughty was an undergraduate student who attended this symposium for academic credit. He offers one student's perspective on the papers presenetd and the effect of these papers on his own perception of the South around him.

Onward and Upward
With the Rising South

GEORGE B. TINDALL

GEORGE B. TINDALL — George B. Tindall, a native South Carolinian, was educated at Furman University and at the University of North Carolina, where he received his doctorate in history in 1951 and where he is now Kenan Professor of History. Tindall has also taught at the University of Mississippi, Eastern Kentucky State College, Women's College of the University of North Carolina, and from 1953 to 1958 at the Louisiana State University.

Since his first major publication, *South Carolina Negroes, 1877-1900*, in 1952, Tindall has authored and edited a number of important books on Southern history, politics, and culture, including *The Disruption of the Solid South* (1972), *A Populist Reader* (1966), *The Pursuit of Southern History: Presidential Addresses of the Southern Historical Association* (1964), and probably most importantly, *The Emergence of the New South, 1913-1945* (1967), which was Volume X of the LSU series *A History of the South*.

For this last volume Tindall received the Jules F. Landry Award of the LSU Press; for *South Carolina Negroes, 1877-1900* he had received Honorable Mention, John H. Dunning Award, given by the American Historical Association. Tindall's scholarly articles have appeared in the *Journal of Southern History, The Journal of Negro History*, the *South Carolina Historical Magazine*, and many other journals and magazines.

Tindall's teaching and scholarship have brought him wide recognition in many forms. He was awarded a Guggenheim Fellowship in 1957, was a Social Science Research Council Fellow in 1959-60, a Visiting Member of the Institute for Advanced Study, Princeton, 1963-64, and a Visiting Fulbright Professor at the University of Vienna, 1967-68.

An active member of the Southern Historical Association, Tindall has held a number of offices in that organization through the years. Upon his election to the presidency he delivered the presidential address "Beyond the Mainstream: The Ethnic Southerners" in 1973.

Tindall is a frequent speaker on topics like "The Rising South," and his keynote address reflects years of study of the rise of the New South and the change the region has gone through since 1945.

It may seem peevish and ungracious to begin a celebration of "The Rising South" on a note of paradox and irony. But one of the occupational hazards of historians is a weakness for skepticism and a sense of kinship with the ancient sage who wrote in the book of Ecclesiastes: "The thing that hath been, it is that which shall be; and that which is done is that which shall be done: and there is no new thing under the sun. . . . There is no remembrance of former things; neither shall there be any remembrance of things that are to come with those that come after."

The symposium on the South is itself a thing that hath been and that which shall be. For among the imponderables and uncertainties of the changing South there seems to be one durable constant—somebody will always be staging a symposium on the changing South. It is one of the flourishing minor industries of the region, one in which countless professional Southerners have built up a vested interest. But it has been a cyclical industry, which fluctuates unpredictably: 1972 was the best year recently, when two major symposia took place within a span of two months, in Tampa and Chapel Hill. The best year of the previous decade was 1965, when the centennial of Appomattox gave rise to a flood of commentaries, including special issues of *Harpers, Look,* and *Newsweek* and a book entitled *The South in Continuity and Change,* issued by the Duke University Press. The most recent such occasion in Tuscaloosa, I believe, was in 1964 when a symposium on "The Deep South in Transformation" celebrated the opening of a new social science building.

If one has a taste for tedium one can trace it back through the musty indexes until the standard title becomes the "New South," that being the subject of a symposium reported in *Review of Reviews* during 1892. With enough perseverance, in fact, one might go on back to those ante-bellum commercial conventions that kept whooping it up for the rising South. Whether this practice had origins in the colonial period, I cannot say, but one should not be surprised to discover that the French Governor Bienville, before he moved from Mobile to New Orleans back in 1718, held a *pourparler* on "Le Sud changeant."

The themes of these colloquies have been constant for at least a century. The standard topics are economics, race, and politics. Industry is rising, the South is becoming urbanized, all this is having profound effects on racial relations and politics. Another consistent theme has been the Vanishing South, forever moving toward the mainstream of American life but somehow never getting there. The Vanishing South, it turns out, has staged one of the most prolonged disappearing acts since the decline and fall of the Roman Empire.

But however clouded the crystal ball may have been, the focus of these confabulations has been clear. The central theme has been change, and the consciousness of change has long been one of the established constants in Southern history. "The people of the South," Vann Woodward wrote in *The Strange Career of Jim Crow*, "should be the last Americans to expect indefinite continuity of their institutions and social arrangements." Consider the transformations that have occurred since Eli Whitney's gin gave rise to the Cotton Kingdom: the westward movement of the cotton belt (eventually to California), the sectional conflict, the rise and fall of the Confederacy, emancipation, the regime of Reconstruction, replaced in turn by that of the New South, which faced down challenge from the Populists, then assimilated the progressives and New Dealers. And consider the changes wrought in the twentieth century by technology, industry, and urbanization. Within three decades the landmarks have toppled in rapid succession: the one-crop agriculture, the one-crop industry, the one-party system, the white primary, the poll tax, racial segregation—indeed so many foundation of the old order that we now live in a post-New South that nobody has yet given a name.

But throughout all the flux of change there have persisted certain dependable constants. Recently an example of one jumped up from the front page of my hometown newspaper, the Greenville *News-Piedmont* for February 17, 1974. A seductive headline ran across the bottom of the front page: "S. C. Piedmont Is Becoming the Energy Capital of the World." In the story that followed and in a sequel the next day the writer asserted: "The potential for economic growth in the Piedmont appears to be unrivaled by any other area in this country and perhaps the world." The reason for this miracle was that Duke Power Company was building a nuclear plant near Gaffney and had another over in Oconee County. Visiting the area of the proposed Cherokee Nuclear Station in a "sparsely populated, undeveloped section of the county," the writer found it obvious "that this area of pine thickets and fields of broomstraw, milkweed, and briars could only benefit by the nearness of the giant power plant with its towering plumed stacks. . . ." He anticipated a new industrial park and a new residential area. If he had ever heard of ecology or the Club of Rome, if he had ever seen the dark satanic mills of Birmingham or felt the rattling rhythm of a weave-room, he did not let on.

Neither, in all likelihood, did he write from a conscious remembrance of former things, but his articles belong to a venerable tradition of the South. They betray a penchant for the superlative that caught the eye of a Harvard historian some years ago. In *The Southern South,* a book published in 1910, historian Albert Bushnell Hart quoted a comment by Walter Hines Page on the "oratorical habit of mind" that had afflicted the postwar generation. "Rousing speech," Page had written, "was more to be desired than accuracy of statement. An exaggerated manner and a tendency to sweeping generalizations were the results." Hart then added his own observation: "Another form of this habit of mind is the love of round numbers, a fondness for stating a thing in the largest terms; thus the clever but no-wise distinguished professor of Latin is 'Probably the greatest classical scholar in the United States,' the siege of Vicksburg was 'the most terrific contest in the annals of warfare,' the material progress of the South is 'the most marvelous thing in human history.' "

It is odd how these habits persist. The booster rhetoric in the Greenville *News-Piedmont* might have been lifted, with slight alteration, from one of those articles the *Manufacturers Record* used to run in the 1920's on the glorious future of hydroelectric "Super-Power," the great "region builder." In fact the sound of the booster rhetoric is about as up-to-date as the music of an Elizabethan ballad or the prose of Sir Walter Raleigh exhorting his countrymen to get in on the New World bonanza. A few years ago, in the journal *Louisiana History,* historian Charles P. Roland remarked on this durable infatuation: the South's persistent sense of destiny, the perennial belief that the region is on the verge of economic fulfillment. Roland began with Lyndon Johnson's proposition that the "crescent of the Gulf offers one of the great opportunities of the Western World"; then he flashed back to Thomas Hariot's report from Roanoke Island that "in short time the planters may . . . enrich themselves and those who trade with them." Then Roland pursued the boosters back to the present, citing along the way, and among others: Hugh Jones, John Lawson, Thomas Jefferson, John C. Calhoun, James H. Hammond, Hinton R. Helper, Henry W. Grady, Francis Dawson, Edwin Mims, Franklin D. Roosevelt, and Walter Prescott Webb. "The South," Roland asserted, "has persistently been the nation's greatest economic enigma—a region of want in the midst of boundless natural riches. It has been, and remains today, a land becoming and not a land become—a garden spot that beckons only to recede like a mirage when approached. It is America's will-o'-the wisp Eden."

One major reason has been the South's fatal affinity for low-wage industries. A few years ago two economists conducted a survey of new plants located in Tennessee between 1955 and 1965. They asked the managers to evaluate the factors that determined their location. The factor most often mentioned and the one assigned the most weight was the low cost and availability of labor. Cheap "Anglo-Saxon" workers are no longer "offered up on the auction block pretty much as their black predecessors were," to quote Broadus Mitchell, at least not so openly. But the Georgia Department of Community Development recently inserted an advertisement in the *Wall Street Journal* that asked: "Is an honest day's work for an honest day's pay an old-fashioned attitude?" The answer was: "Not in Georgia. In our smaller towns, you'll find people who are eager to work. . . . Manpower is one of our State's greatest assets." The words are unimpeachable, but what lies between the lines is something else again.

Of course there is a dilemma for the South in this predicament. Even sweatshops, sad to relate, may give a leg up to displaced field hands. One must learn to crawl before he can walk, and any balanced picture of Southern development must show the vistas of opportunity that have opened in the past. Millions of Southerners, most often white but sometimes black, have moved up from farm to mill village and town, from tenancy or yeomanry to middle-class affluence. A review of statistics will show that, at least since 1880, industrial development in the region has moved at a faster pace than in the nation at large and that the gap between North and South continues to narrow.

Per capita income has followed a similar path. Excluding Texas and Oklahoma, which would have made the averages still higher, per capita incomes that were only 69.1 percent of the national average in 1959 had reached 73 percent in 1963 and 81 percent in 1970. The out-migration that has made the South historically a seedbed of population for the rest of the country has been reversed since the mid-1950's. During the 1960's the South had a total net in-migration of nearly 500,000 despite a new loss of nearly 1½ million blacks.

By the 1950's the region scored its urban breakthrough. By 1960 the population was 58 percent urban and by 1970, 64.6 percent urban. And only a small part of the remainder were still farming. In the states of the former Confederacy in 1964, only about 8 percent of the population remained on farms—about 3.8 million Southerners. And farming has undergone sweeping changes. "The bizarre incident of the New Deal plow-up in 1933," historian Tom Clark wrote, "closed the ledger on an era of Southern history that began with Eli Whitney." In 1969, the South was growing only about 79 percent of the nation's cotton, and the crop fetched only about 7 percent of the total worth of

Southern farm products. Poultry and eggs accounted for nearly three times as much, cattle for nearly four times as much, cattle and dairy products combined for nearly five times as much. Green pastures and elongated hencoops have become features of the landscape as common as the endless rows of cotton used to be. If the streams still run muddy, it is because of building projects rather than eroded fields.

There are some other gratifying features in the new landscape. Being late to develop, Southern industry has escaped the urgent need to converge on power sources and railheads. Electricity, petroleum, and natural gas can go by cable or pipeline, the products can go by truck, and the mills can straggle across the landscape. The idyllic vision of factory-farm living has become reality for many and should prevail widely so long as the gasoline holds out. But nobody who has driven through the Southern Ruhr Valley along the Mississippi between Baton Rouge and New Orleans, and nobody who has fought his way through the shabby strips that lead to Southern cities can be unaware of greater pitfalls ahead.

An even more desperate consequence of change is an abomination that keeps away from the sight of comfortable people, like the dark side of the moon, the multitudes left stranded in the backwaters of economic development. Five years ago, after Senator Ernest M. Hollings, Jr., had toured some of the rural slums down home in South Carolina, he admitted to a Senate committee that as governor he had supported "The public policy of covering up the problem of hunger" in the interest of attracting new industry and creating jobs. "I know the need for jobs," he said, "but what I am talking about here . . . is downright hunger. The people I saw couldn't possibly work."

Perhaps better planning could help bring about more rational development, but it affords no panacea. Even so enlightened an enterprise as the Tennessee Valley Authority has become a voracious consumer of strip-mined coal and has come under attack for other sins against the public. It is an old experience that public regulatory agencies tend to fall under the sway of those they are supposed to restrain. Vested interests and real-estate promoters repeatedly bend planning boards to their own purposes.

Years ago the New Deal offered funds to encourage the development of planning agencies. By 1935 all the Southern governors had appointed planning boards, and by 1938 all the boards had statutory authority. Their purpose, as the Arkansas planners put it in 1936, was the "common sense principle of directing the future physical development of a state in accordance with a comprehensive long-term coordinated plan" that would "take into account many social and economic considerations." In 1940 the governors of seven states set up the Southeastern Regional Planning Commission to correlate the program.

But planning took a low priority. The state boards had scarcely moved beyond general surveys when the pressure for payrolls caused their transformation into development boards. So agencies that started with some promise of broad-gauged social planning ended as agencies to lure the vagrant factories. Maybe the movement came forty years too soon and maybe new payrolls were what a backward region most desperately needed, but the momentum for planning was lost.

The ironies of history that overtake the best-laid plans—the hopes unfulfilled, the reversal of trends, the unexpected turns of fortune—these ironies have unfolded once again in the movements for black liberation. The changes in racial relations, of course, have produced the most vivid human drama in the recent South, and the most emotionally wrenching. Surely, one may think, these things must be unparalleled in the Southern past: the dramatic confrontations, the new legal rights attained by black Southerners, the sudden collapse of massive resistance, and the turn to more subtle forms of white resistance.

In 1974, here in the state of Alabama, the South's leading segregationist won renomination for governor after a campaign in which he openly courted the black vote. In 1963 he had cast down the gauntlet and proclaimed: "Segregation now, segregation forever." Forever, it turned out, lasted about ten years. But as Harold Wilson has said, one week is a long time in politics.

Such a sudden collapse of resistance had occurred before, in the far more wrenching drama of emancipation. And according to historian Clement Eaton, "One of the most striking aspects of the Southern mood after Appomattox was the widespread expression of approval, even relief, that slavery had been abolished. Ex-Governor Henry A. Wise of Virginia, for example, declared in an open address on June 17, 1873, before Roanoke College that slavery was the worst curse that had ever rested on the Southern people and that it had been a great incubus on Southern development."

The threat to segregation, like the threat to slavery, however, brought forth a stubborn defense. The White Citizens' Councils, for example, had their counterparts in the vigilance committees of the Old South. The effort to justify segregation revived many points of the proslavery argument, in altered form. The doctrine of interposition revived, or sought to revive, an old doctrine of state rights. But the resistance to civil rights proved to be a pale replica of the resistance to abolition, perhaps because Southerners recognized the truth of what Governor Earl Long told the Louisiana legislature: They had to realize that the Feds have got the A-bomb now.

Historians always protest reluctance to don the robes of prophecy, but they protest too much, because they are always doing it under the guise of showing trends from the past. In a paper first delivered twenty years ago and published in 1960 under the title, "The Central Theme Revisited," I suggested that the spell cast by the old Southern Credo on race and the widespread assumption that it was the central explanation of Southern character obscured the equally fundamental role of its antithesis, the American Creed of equality, which a white Southerner defined in 1776. "Thus criticism of southern racial practice has repeatedly generated temporary intransigence, but in the long run and more significantly it has also compelled self-justification and a slow but steady adjustment by white Southerners in the direction of the American faith in equality of opportunity and rights." This is not, of course, to ignore other factors—religious, social, ideological, economic, and political—that have contributed to the white adjustment.

Black reactions have evinced historical parallels too. The Montgomery bus boycott, which began a long sequence of dramatic confrontations, had its counterpart in the streetcar boycotts that protested the imposition of Jim Crow requirements at the turn of the century. The new legal rights won in court decisions and in the climactic Civil Rights and Voting Rights Acts had their counterparts and much of their basis in the Reconstruction Amendments, which lay dormant through the later reaction but came back to life in the twentieth century.

The millennial hopes and the Biblical rhetoric of Martin Luther King's civil rights movement had their parallels in the crusade against slavery. Both maintained a high level of moral exaltation, which could not last indefinitely, but both, in fact, achieved their objectives of fixing certain principles in the law of the land, if not yet in the practice of the land. Each of the former institutions left its shadow to haunt posterity. Slavery, in the guise of peonage, still lingers in the boondocks. Segregation, in the guise of the Christian academy, flourishes today. Emancipation freed the slaves but failed to deliver forty acres and a mule. Civil rights opened up the restaurants but failed ot provide for the check.

In the aftermath of slavery, tenancy and the failure of the Freedmen's Savings Bank taught paradoxical lessons in the improvidence of thrift and the value of living for the day—before somebody took it away from you. In the aftermath of segregation, the urban ghetto taught lessons in brigandage and looting—because nobody was going to give it to you. At least the latter expressed a revolution of rising expectations. The Civil Rights Act of 1964, moreover, set up a ban on discrimination in jobs and education, that, in turn, has brought on programs to provide special restitution for the deprivations of the past. However ill-designed they may be in some instances, these things go well beyond the transient relief offered by the Freedman's Bureau after the Civil War. Their legality, however, remains an unsettled question. The Supreme Court has so far dodged a resolution of the issue.

Disappointment with the gains achieved by emancipation and civil rights left a heritage of disillusionment, and the discontent in each case gave rise to movements that turned inward upon the black community: first Booker T. Washington and his policy of accommodation, vocational studies, and self-help; more recently black power and a policy of defiance, black studies, and separatism. More than one white has confessed puzzlement at the ramifications of the black power movement and has asked in unconscious echo of Sigmund Freud's question about women: "What do they want?" Surely nobody, white or black, has the definitive answer, but historical perspectives suggest that black power gives a new name and a new manifestation to what used to be called Negro nationalism, an undercurrent that has always moved in the black community and that has surfaced most conspicuously in two mass movements of the twentieth century: Marcus Garvey's back-to-Africa crusade of the 1920's and the separatist movement to which Stokely Carmichael gave the name "black power" in 1966.

The movements shared a common slogan, "Black is beautiful," and a common fear that integration would destroy black identity. Both have had their chief seat in the urban North and both have had among their most conspicuous leaders natives of the West Indies, where a continuing sense of identification with black Africa has nourished the social myth of *négritude*.

At some point, however, the parallels begin to break down and the connecting lines begin to cross over one another. Sometimes black power looks like Booker T. Washington warmed over and spiced up with a dash of Karl Marx—or is it Marcus Garvey warmed over and spiced up with a dash of Marshall McLuhan? Or more appropriately, perhaps, is it two strange mixtures of Washington the accommodationist and his old adversary, W. E. B. Du Bois, the egalitarian. The formula for black power seems to mix equal portions of Washington's self-help and Du Bois's proud defiance, while the recipe for integration seems to mix equal portions of Washington's restraint and Du Bois's quest for equal rights.

In retrospect, however, Washington and Du Bois emerge less

as the champions of incompatible philosophies than as the complementary leaders of a common struggle carried on at two levels, the one laying a foundation for the growing success of the other's approach. Can it be that eventually the integrationists and separatists of the present will emerge as the complementary poles of a similar dialectic, moving toward a synthesis already dimly seen: an ongoing ethnic identity within an integrated society, so that being an Afro-American will be something like being an Irish-American or a Polish-American—or, for that matter, a Southern-white-American? Such an outcome might combine the best of both worlds, achieving cultural and psychological fulfillment without discarding political and economic goals.

It has become common now to speak of a First and Second Reconstruction, the two occurring about a century apart. They were alike in achieving certain goals and alike in the disillusionment and reaction that followed. They seem to have been different in their political effects, however: one destroyed the chances for a two-party system, the other seems to have improved the chances. Yet, although the tides move in a different direction now, the politics of the South have come back into a state of flux something like that which existed in the lost years before the triumph of Jim Crow and the Solid South at the turn of the century. Southern politics are open once again to the strategies of coalition that Presidents Hayes, Garfield, Arthur, and Harrison tried to exploit, but with little success.

After Reconstruction every Southern strategy failed the Republicans: first the effort by Hayes to enlist Southern conservatives, then the effort by Garfield and Arthur to enlist Southern insurgents. The stigma of Reconstruction, however unfair it may have been, was too much to overcome, and the party ceased to offer effective opposition except in parts of the upper South.

Ever since the 1920's, however, new conditions have caused repeated disruptions of Southern Democracy: the clash between metropolitan and rural values in 1924 and 1928, sectional tensions aroused by the New Deal, the shift of black voters to the Democratic party, and the rise of the civil rights movement. The Dixie-

crat rebellion marked the end of the Solid South in the electoral
college.

With the election of Dwight D. Eisenhower in 1952, Hayes's
strategy at last succeeded. The beneficiary of a kind of "conservative chic" in the burgeoning suburbs, Eisenhower also garnered a
sizeable black vote and carried several states of the outer South.
Nixon's vote in 1960, although smaller, followed the same pattern,
but Goldwater in 1964 and Nixon in 1968 and after gave the
Southern strategy a new twist.

Abandoning the black vote (once traditionally Republican)
just as it was on the rise and combining Hayes's appeal to conservatives with Arthur's appeal to insurgents, Goldwater and Nixon
wooed simultaneously the silk-stockinged suburbanites and the
rebellious segregationists. Both encountered trouble—Goldwater
in suburbia and Nixon in Wallace country—and whether such
an unlikely coalition can long endure remains to be seen, and at
what cost to the party of the Great Emancipator.

Democrats, however, had been able to hold plebeian and
patrician in the same party for many years. The South, "more
than any other part of the country, retains the idea of the Gentry
versus the Lower Classes," Sinclair Lewis wrote in 1929 after
visiting the scene of the strike at Marion, North Carolina. But
he added: "It doesn't take much to feel that you are in the Gentry.
Owning a small grocery . . .will do it." In the New South, as in
the Old, one did not have to share the power of the elite in order
to share the mystique.

One of the neglected areas of recent Southern history, George
Mowry has said, is this persistent "elite and its relationship to the
area's politicians." Even such an expert on Southern politics as
V. O. Key, Jr., Mowry noted, had to be equivocal on the subject
for want of clear knowledge. The result of the existing system,
however, was more certain: "a social and economic structure in
which the gulf between the rich and the poor has been extra-
ordinarily wide." The record, Mowry said, "is written in beating
back the twin threats of liberal or progressive state governments
and of labor unions, in maintaining the wage differentials between

classes within the South, and by comparison to those existing elsewhere in the nation, and in holding to a minimum federal intervention in either the industrial or the racial question." At least for a long time. And the two questions were connected: "sustained racial passions meant one-party government, one-party government meant upper-class control, and hence antiunion government, Q. E. D.: a certain level of racial animosity worked to the benefit of the owning classes."

Nevertheless, within the last twenty years Republicans have created a durable opposition in the South for the first time since the heyday of the Whigs in the 1840's. With the rise of a two-party system, therefore, Southern politics seem headed toward a more structured arrangement than in the past, with an electorate, now unburdened of the old restrictions, drawn into greater participation by party competition. The new situation has opened Southern politics to a wider range of possibilities.

The outcome depends largely upon the directions taken by those groups that have felt most aggrieved in the recent past: the five million or so Wallace voters and the five million or so black voters. The variant possibilities are highlighted by the recent experience of the two cities that elected black members of Congress in 1972. In Houston a coalition of blacks with plebeian whites has developed while in Atlanta black politicians have gained support among the white elite. Either way coalition politics enhance the chances for reconciliation between the races and bear out the judgment of Rutherford B. Hayes long ago that a division in the white vote would provide the best protection of black civil rights.

Accounts of Maynard Jackson's inauguration as mayor of Atlanta almost persuade one that there is a new thing under the sun after all. At least we have come a long way from those malicious pictures of black Sambo in the Reconstruction legislature with a cigar in his face and his feet on the desk. The installation of Atlanta's black mayor may have been the most elegant political event ever staged in the South. The mayor's aunt, Mattiwilda Dobbs, presented spirituals and an operatic aria, and the Atlanta Symphony under Robert Shaw presented the choral finale of Beethoven's Ninth Symphony, which sets to music the triumphant words of Schiller's "Ode to Joy": *Alle Menschen werden Bruder.* All mankind shall be brothers. And to go from the sublime to the ridiculous, as it were, one might tune in the latest country music sensation, Tanya Tucker, singing "I Believe the South Is Gonna Rise Again": "A brand-new breeze is blowin' cross the Southland," it goes, "And I see a brand new kind of brotherhood."

Wide vistas of opportunity beckon at last, and if a leadership can emerge with the genius to seize the day the South can exploit a chance that comes to few generations. Reconciliation is not out of reach, the land remains relatively unspoiled, the political system is more open and unrestricted than ever before. It may be something of a cliché now, but it is also a self-evident truth that a region so late in developing has a chance to learn from the mistakes of others. What Lewis Mumford said twenty-five years ago remains almost as true today as it was then: "Most of the measures that must be taken in the South may be of a positive rather than a remedial nature; they are matters of preserving a balance that still exists, rather than of re-establishing a balance that has been almost utterly destroyed."

But before this begins to sound like Henry Grady warmed over and spiced up with a dash of Pollyanna, let us not forget that if experience is any guide, the South will blow it. We shall have to make the same mistakes all over again, and we shall achieve the urban blight, the crowding, the traffic jams, the slums, the ghettoes, the pollution, the frenzy, and all the other ills that modern man is heir to. We are already well on the way. And to say that a different outcome depends upon a leadership with the genius to seize the day, to say that after Watergate, why that is a sobering thought.

The Union Contribution

BARNEY WEEKS

BARNEY WEEKS—Barney Weeks, a native of Alabama, was first elected president of the Alabama Labor Council, AFL-CIO, in 1957 and has been reelected every two years since then. Week's career in organized labor began with his employment by several Alabama newspapers. He was elected president of the Montgomery Typographical Union, an officer of the Montgomery Central Labor Union, and then vice-president of the Alabama Labor Council, AFL-CIO, which job he held at the time of his election to the presidency. During World War II Weeks served in the European Theater in the Corps of Engineers and in Ordnance School.

Active in community affairs and in state and local politics, he is a member of the National Defense Executive Reservists, The Office of Economic Opportunity Labor Advisory Committee, and he is a past member of the Southeastern Regional Manpower Advisory Committee and of the Regional Health Advisory Committee for HEW. He presently serves on the Executive Committee of the AFL-CIO Appalachian Council and the AFL-CIO Committee on State and Local Central Bodies and is vice-president of the Alabama Consumers Association, president of the Southern Labor School, and treasurer of the Alabama Association for Mental Health.

Weeks is a direct and persuasive advocate for the union movement in the state of Alabama.

The rather phenomenal growth of organized labor in the South over the past three decades has played an important and correlating role in the upswing of the Southern economy. The two—expanding union organization and continuing economic progress—have gone hand in hand. With them, unions have brought higher paying jobs, greater economic security, and less out-migration of the workforce.

Collectively, unions have contributed greatly to Alabama's transformation from a farm to an industrial economy. Today, Alabama

—once thought of as a land of cotton and small farms—is the most unionized state percentagewise in the Southeast. Its steel mills are the largest south of Pittsburgh. Its rubber factories make the state the nation's second largest producer of passenger tires. Its mines supply big percentages of the nation's coal, mica, and bauxite. Alabama's nonfarm workforce now totals 1,138,000, an economic benchmark that puts the state in the big leagues as a producer and retailer for the nation's markets. Some 350,000 Alabamians work directly in the factories; another 10,000 are employed in mining operations; 61,000 are in construction; 62,000 in transportation, communications, and utilities; 221,300 in wholesale and retail trade positions; and 230,000 on government payrolls.

Today, Alabama factory workers average $148 a week, or $3.62 an hour, ranking them favorably among their coworkers in the other Southeastern states. Factory workers in Birmingham—where union influence is strong—do even better at $4.29 an hour, or $175 a week, higher than any other Southeastern city.

It is undisputed that unions bring a higher share of company profits to the workers themselves, who in turn spend their wages at home, generate higher state and local tax revenues, and contribute to the overall progress of the community. That is why the longer industrialized, more heavily union towns and cities of the Northeast and Midwest have prospered earlier and have attracted many of our Southern workers.

While it is true that unions were slow to organize in the South, some of the most intense union activity in the nation is now being carried on in Dixie. In the six-year period from 1964 to 1970, for instance, the eight Southeastern states added almost a half million workers (according to the U.S. Bureau of Labor Statistics) to the organized workforce, jumping the total from 1,144,000 to 1,572,000. Alabama today can lay claim to more than 228,000 union workers, a big majority of whom are members of the AFL-CIO. That is a far cry from the 25,000 or so who carried union cards in Alabama in 1900 or the 65,000 in 1940.

Union presence on a major scale was not felt in Alabama until the industrial boom years encompassing World War II and the Korean War. During the years from 1939 to 1953 several Southern states, including Alabama, gained more than 100,000 new union members. In that fourteen-year span, Alabama jumped from 64,000 union workers in 1939 to 168,000 in 1953, for an increase of 104,000; Georgia went from 36,000 to 136,000 (up 100,000); Tennessee from 71,000 to 187,000 (up 116,000); Kentucky from 85,000 to 155,000 (up 70,000); Virginia from 68,000 to 156,000 (up 88,000); Florida from 44,000 to 136,000 (up 92,000); and Louisiana from 38,000 to 136,000 (up 98,000). During the same period, North Carolina jumped from 26,000 to 84,000 (up 58,000); South Carolina from 12,000 to 50,000 (up 38,000); Mississippi from 13,000 to 50,000 (up 37,000); and Arkansas from 25,000 to 60,000 (up 35,000).

In some of the border states the increases were even more dramatic: Maryland went from 59,000 at the start of World War II in 1939 to 204,000 in 1953, when the Korean War came to a close. Texas also leaped ahead, going from 111,000 in 1939 to 375,000 union workers in 1953, up a whopping 264,000 and bettering even the Maryland increase of 145,000. All this is to say that Southern unionism really got its foot in the door during the war years and has been growing—though at a slower pace— ever since.

Despite the growth of the trade union movement in the South and the great influx of new industry that preceded it, the Southern states still badly trail the nation in that most important of economic indicators—per capita income. The Center for Southern Studies at Duke University reports that, although the South led the nation in growth during the 1960's, it still ranks as the poorest region in the country. And, the Duke investigation further reports, the gap between the rich and the poor is greater in the South than anywhere else in the nation. Additionally, J. Ray Marshall, a professor at the University of Texas, has found that 46 percent of the country's poor live in the South although the region has only 21 percent of the total population.

In 1970 the South's average per capita personal income was

$3,062, 78 percent of the national average of $3,910. Although this was better than the 50 percent of the national average the South showed in 1930 and the 60 percent in 1940, it shows that we, as a region, still have a long way to go.

In a poll of ten Southern states, not a single state had an income level that reached the national average in 1972. The poorest state in the South in per capita income was Mississippi with $3,137, while Virginia was the richest with $4,298. Alabama placed eighth among southern states with $3,420—$1,072 under the 1972 national average. Average per capita income in Southern states that year was $3,801; the national average hit $4,492.

After the Civil War and into the twentieth century, we Southerners talked a lot about the "New South" and tried to emulate the industrial model of the Northeast. Despite some significant breakthroughs in the rush to get into the industrial picture, there developed one serious flaw in the game plan. Southern industry was financed by Northern capitalists seeking a short-term payoff without regard for long-term effects on the South's human and natural resources. The South failed to develop a class of entrepreneurs of its own that would take a long-range view toward the region's economic development. The Morgans, Mellons, Rockefellers sent their agents to take charge of the South's railroads, mines, ironworks, and financial corporations. The Southern economy came to be one of branch plants, branch banks, captive mines, and chain stores. What came was low-wage, low-value-creating industry. For the most part it located near the source of supply of raw materials, and, when this was exploited, it closed shop and moved elsewhere. In their zeal to attract new industry—any industry—many Southern developers unwittingly aided in the location of bad corporate citizens who were just as anxious to exploit the local labor force as the natural resources.

Faced with a continuing poor economy despite such new industry, the governors of sixteen Southern and border states met in Nashville in 1962 to discuss the problem that plagued them all. Why, the governors asked, did the South's per capita income continue to trail the national average despite such impressive economic and industrial growth? The governors pondered the problem and came up with this answer: Most of the industries that have come to the South pay low wages. If the South would replace low-wage industries with plants that pay high wages, per capita income would catch up with the national average and the South would prosper.

A special study of the Southern Governor's Conference stated:

> We suggest that the reason the annual per capita income of Southern workers in manufacturing is $800 below that of workers in the non-South is our past reliance on industries in which the wages are at the bottom of the list.
>
> It is well-known, for example, that weekly wages in apparel, leather and textiles are near the bottom in weekly wage rates while machinery, transportation equipment and chemicals, along with paper, petroleum and coal, are substantially above the average.
>
> Therefore, our future industrial development offers other opportunities to further strengthen the region's economic position through the selection of industries which offer our people a more substantial wage.

The governors said that the solution to this basic low-wage problem revolves around the South being "more selective in the types of industries being established in the region." The South should, they resolved, "cease shooting with a shotgun to bag any and all enterprises in their future industrial promotion efforts, but rather use the rifle approach in order to interest industries paying high wages."

In their analysis twelve years ago, the governors omitted one factor that may be of importance in inhibiting economic growth, namely the so-called "right-to-work" laws. They failed to examine the widespread prevalence of antilabor legislation, typified by the "right-to-work" laws, and of antilabor community attitudes that for many years have been used as "bait" to lure low-wage, runaway industries into the South—the type of industries the Southern governors so bitterly decried in Nashville. Of the eighteen "right-to-work" states, ten are in the South and Alabama is one of them. These laws were purposefully enacted in most states of the South to perpetuate sharecropper wages and to make it difficult, if not impossible, for Southern workers to organize effectively and to participate in the collective bargaining process through representation by responsible labor unions. The existence of strong labor unions in the non-"right-to-work" states, it should be pointed out, is equated with the high wages the Southern governors said they wanted for their workers.

Nor did the governors ask whether "right-to-work" laws and kindred antilabor legislation are a factor in the flight of the Southern labor force, both skilled and unskilled, to regions of the nation where labor-management relations are not clouded by these antilabor laws, one of the fruits of which has been industrial unrest.

I suggest that the Southern governors, in their search for higher wage industries, overlooked one of the facets of their economic problem by failing to give recognition to the need for removing "right-to-work" laws and other antilabor legislation from their statute books. One of the most progressive steps Alabama could take would be to repeal its 1953 "Right-To-Work" Law, which has inhibited growth in this state long enough. It was never designed to protect the worker who did not want to join the union that had organized his plant. What it did was to so weaken the union's strength that it could not obtain equal footing with management in labor disputes.

Preoccupation with the "bait" aspect of "right-to-work" laws by some well-meaning but all too eager industry seekers produced some surprises on the part of unimpressed corporations. First of all the "right-to-work" concept is an idea out of step with today's brand of labor-management relations. It is a misnomer of the worst sort. Responsible industry these days pretty much realizes that if it has labor trouble in one state, it is quite likely to have it wherever it goes. In fact, many major manufacturing groups have gone to a system of industry-wide bargaining that cuts across state and even regional lines. Some manufacturers, like steel, bargain on a national basis. For this reason industry looks for a supply of skilled labor along with favorable labor-management relations when it makes a move. More and more this means one where workers—through collective bargaining—have some real input into the industry itself and have a stake in high productivity.

A University of North Carolina study on the effect of "right-to-work" laws on Southern industry concludes:

> In sum, there is no evidence that industry as a whole is concerned with "right-to-work" laws when selecting a location for expansion. Of the 10 states which led in the percentage of increased industrialization from 1939 to 1953 (the period of greatest union growth in the South), only two, Texas and Florida, were right-to-work states.
>
> Those industries which are either market or supply oriented, the industries which create the largest number of jobs and pay the highest wages, prefer a high-wage to a low-wage area.
>
> It is only those industries such as apparel, shoe and textile which concern themselves wth a right-to-work law and these are the industries which create rather than solve problems.
>
> If a low wage scale is the only enticement which the Southeastern states have to offer new industry, they might as well be reconciled to a status of permanent economic colonialism. The use of low-wage Southern labor to produce products for sale in a national market represents an exploitation that is just as destructive as an irresponsible mining of natural resources. . . . Such exploitation takes the form of extracting the energies of a state without replacement and without proper compensation.
>
> There is nothing desirable about industrialization per se. Industrialization, accompanied by low wages, is the cause, not the cure, for economic problems.

Another possible side effect of the "right-to-work" laws has been the continued, wholesale migration of skilled workers from the South to non-"right-to-work" states in search of higher wages, greater security, and better working conditions. The U.S. Labor Department reports that in the 1950's no less than five million persons moved to a different state, and the largest outflow was from the South. It is fair to say that job changing was the most important influence affecting this movement.

The out-migration figures show just how tragic the drain on Alabama's human resources has been. In the decade from 1950 to

1960, a total of 368,000 persons left the state to live elsewhere. In the next decade, 1960-70, the figure was reduced to 233,000—better but still tragic.

A report just out from the Center for Business and Economic Research at The University of Alabama says that from 1965 to 1970, the state suffered net losses of 72,646, three-fourths of that number black. During that five-year period, for instance, 12,151 Alabama blacks moved to Michigan, many no doubt to find jobs in the automobile plants. More than 7,000 each went to such places as Ohio, California, and New York, all high-wage, heavy industry states with no "right-to-work" laws.

From the census figures, it is apparent that many if not most of those leaving the state came off the farm. Alabama's farm population dropped from 960,000 in 1950 to 519,000 in 1960 to 216,000 in 1970. Since the some 200,000 farm people in Alabama today produce more than the nearly one million did twenty-four years ago, the loss must be calculated in human resource terms rather than in crop production.

However, some realistic planning and a more sincere effort to reverse the continuing loss of Alabama citizenry has begun to take hold. Rural job opportunities—including the location of manufacturing plants in small counties—have increased appreciably in recent years. Government assistance, such as the Rural Development Act of 1972, has also proven beneficial. More business leaders have expanded their location of plants, offices, laboratories, and distribution centers in the countryside. And more cities and towns have cut down on their promotion of industrial and population growth.

While the Southern region is now experiencing a period of population adjustment—from out-migration to a net gain of population—an outflow of people is still expected in some states. For example, Alabama is expected to show a net migration loss of 1.4 percent in the 1980—85 period; Mississippi, 3.2 percent and West Virginia, 1.5 percent.

Economically, however, things are looking up for the Southern region. Many Southern businessmen and labor leaders believe the region will not remain a low-wage, little-unionized area for long. In their view the pace and diversification of industrialization will dictate changes, plus the fact that the South has developed to the point where it need no longer court industries seeking cheap labor. Furthermore, some leaders believe that it is necessary to upgrade the standard of living for more of the population than has been done thus far.

Dial Murphy, national representative in Houston for the Oil, Chemical & Atomic Workers International Union, sums up one widely held view:

> There will inevitably be greater unionization. The day of cheap labor is coming to a close because industrialization is generating a greater demand for labor, which means more competition for labor and more compensation.

William Weaver, president of the National Life & Accident Company in Nashville, says:

> The day is over when we must seek sweat-shop labor in order to get jobs. What we want to attract now are higher-paying, capital-intensive industries.

Alabama has experienced some success in this area of late. Included among our very newest industries are an $80 million General Motors plant going up in Limestone County and a $200 million chemical works that is being built by a German manufacturer in Mobile. Overall last year, the governor's office announced that capital investment for new and expanded Alabama industry reached a record $1.7 billion. The figure includes 164 new plants and 841 expansions of existing industry. Together, the state estimates, the boom of 1973 may produce as many as 42,998 new job opportunities upon completion.

Alabama—and the South—seems to have a unique opportunity now to capitalize on the past experience of other regions and build an even better future. A recent book on the South, *You Can't Eat Magnolias,* reads in part:

> The test for the South is whether it can take hold of the energy

of industrialization and urbanization and shape it into a more graceful, more humane and more livable environment than in other regions.

Only time, of course, will tell. Of one thing I am certain. The labor movement in Alabama will continue to be productive and to make a significant and needed contribution to bettering the lot of all workers. Its influence on selective, high-pay industry will continue to be pressed, and its zeal and desire for democracy in the workplaces, dignity on the job, decent wages, and improved working conditions will not diminish but grow stronger. Unions exist not to tear down but to build up. Our goal is to build a better Alabama. We have been fairly successful in the past. We plan even greater breakthroughs in the future.

The Fragile, Threatened
Landscapes of the South

VERDA HORNE

VERDA HORNE—Verda Horne's lifelong interest in the study and preservation of natural life began in her native state of Utah where she taught
and conducted research in biology at her alma mater, Utah State. Horne
went on to graduate study at the University of Minnesota and was Minneapolis-St. Paul director of the Federal Writers Project, preparing the *Guide
to the State* series of state-by-state biological studies.

Since moving to Alabama more than thirty-five years ago, Horne has
continued her research and has taught in public and private schools at all
levels. She has taught at the University of South Alabama, where she was
director of the Office of Publications, and at Spring Hill College in Mobile.

Horne served for eight years on the World Service Committee. She is
a charter member and on the board of the Alabama Conservancy, a charter
member and on the board of the National Trails Council, and she is the
Alabama League of Women Voters Chairman for Environmental Quality.
Horne is a member of the Mobile County Environmental Education Advisory Council on Environmental Quality in Education and the Environmental Advisory Council of the Alabama Department of Education.

She is presently completing her work as head of the Alabama Commission on Public Issues. The primary focus of that commission was the
problems of land management and the environment of the poor.

Horne initiated the William Bartram National Scenic and Historical Trail
proposal and in this essay her interests in preserving both our historical
and our natural heritage are wed.

The use of the land will be an issue at least for the remainder of
my life. I may be forgiven, then, if I put my contribution to this
series in the context of the uses of the land. However, I have
chosen as my title "The Fragile, Threatened Landscapes of the
South."

I am convinced that fair access to living space and access to

35

work and work space, under conditions consistent with physical
and mental health, will be demanded by all people on this planet
before the end of this century. I am convinced, also, that with a
continuation of our present arrangements we shall not be able to
meet those demands. Whether or not our present patterns can be
modified sufficiently to allow for world-wide adjustment I do not
know. I envy those younger than I who are free to learn, to act, to
lead, and to experiment and who will have much to say about the
outcome.

I have chosen to discuss one facet of the danger that threatens
us—the danger of destroying those parts of the physical world
that one day might provide not only mankind's physical sustenance
and shelter but mankind's spiritual and emotional needs as well.
All over this planet small groups are trying to measure the capacity
of the earth to meet the needs of earth's populations and the
capacity of mankind to adjust to that capacity.

In Africa do we keep a hippopotamus alive if, when he emerges
from the waterhole, he tramples the crops upon which a village
must feed? Or do we save a herd of caribou in the Arctic and
delay the delivery of oil to far-off consumers? Do we deny our
appetite for beef in order to share fertilizer with starving people
unable to buy it at the going rate?

The chips are down; the questions won't wait. I shall not try
to answer them; my generation produced the tools and techniques
that brought the question to issue. Instead of pretending to offer
panaceas, I shall suggest, instead, some procedures that might enable us to hold some options open for the future use of our
physical world.

Waste, even hidden waste, will, I am certain, disappear. Solar
power, natural systems energy, and even nuclear power will one
day comfort us, but not as soon as we need them. Some of the
threatened deprivations do not frighten me. I have lived with
many of them, and so, one day, will everyone. But our need for
the earth in all its diverse patterns, in all its multifarious moods,
we shall give up only to our great deprivation. It is of some
remnants of that natural world and their meaning for us that I

write. Their protection, in dollars, is infinitesimal; the cost in work and wisdom may be beyond our capacity, but I have hopes. I am convinced that 1973-74 marks a very great shift in national and international perspective, that the shift in personal perspective likewise has changed for many of us as it will for all of us, if not this year, then certainly before this decade is over.

The rapidity with which these changes occur, being unpredictable and uneven, make accommodations in institutions, governments, and professions most difficult. Since I count myself a humanist and a naturalist, I am concerned that we do what we can to ameliorate some of the destructive effects of our adjustments, both personal and professional. Problems arise from our seeming mania to assure ourselves continued access to the supplies and paraphernalia required to maintain our so-called life-style. Although energy comes first to mind, there are other resource shortages, and in most of them the land is likely to be the loser.

Mankind did not begin to change the physical world in this generation nor in this century. Physical alteration is an old, old story, and much of the damage has been irreversible. It is acceleration of change that now we fear—acceleration due to more hands and far more effective and destructive tools.

A century or more ago, a young American stood, as we stand today, trying to determine how he and his neighbors had managed to make barren the green hills of Vermont's landscape. "Marsh had witnessed a whole cycle of deterioration. Not even in the tobacco and cotton lands of the South were forests removed and soils exhausted faster than on the Green Mountain slopes. When insects, disease, and competition put an end to wheat raising and Vermonters turned to sheep, their close-grazing flocks completed the hillside devastation."[1]

I want to dwell a bit longer on this man, George Perkins Marsh, and his life work. He pursued his education in law in fitful bits, for his chosen school, Dartmouth, was involved in a still famous law case. He dealt in lumber and other trades, he learned and taught Latin and Greek, he mastered twenty other languages, he knew almost every learned man in Europe and America, yet the effect of man on the land haunted him until he died at the age of eighty-one. I shall describe, also, the legacy of three other men, all early visitors to Alabama. They too, like Marsh, found here some unusual values and places that we, to whom these places are more familiar, might overlook or fail to protect. Finally, I shall make what I consider a modest proposal that should be discussed and, perhaps, implemented before our day ends short and the fragile remnants of our landscape have disappeared.

Why do I do so? Quite simply, I view mankind's journey through the finite world as a tenuous, uneven, and wavering one. I cannot forget, nor do I ever wish to forget, the horror my generation felt in those frightening days when Adolph Hitler burned the books in the libraries of his homeland in order to rid his nation of the ideas those books recorded or proclaimed. I still imagine I hear the radioed sounds of those crackling fires.

To those of you who belong to this generation, accustomed to the endless spewing of the copier, the terror of book burning may have lost its edge. But many of you have shared the concern about the disappearance of the wild places, not only the vast wildernesses but the tiny pockets of the natural world. "Nature," we often say, "is an open book." Perhaps there is a parallel with book burning when we close forever a page of nature's book.

Necessary as is some of this conversion and revision of our natural world to our biological and social needs, we may question whether some of this progress may, indeed, be linked to poverty in a way Henry George could not have guessed. So I am concerned with our witless compulsion, now that the tools are in our hands, to uproot, bury, or burn that book of nature that we proclaim lies open for all to read.

I could attempt some estimates of costs and gains of these transformations, of options disappearing or emerging, but I shall not do so. There are professional guides who can document the tally to the millimicron, the millirem, the cubic mile, the light year. Not all gains are measurable, nor all losses. There are other values to be considered—aesthetic, emotional, humane.

Some of you have watched the eagle build its nest, as I have.

You, too, may have seen the painted bunting in its psychedelic colors, followed the ptarmigan on a windy peak, the alligator in a dark bayou. Or perhaps you have touched the giant redwood still green-topped after two centuries.

We who have stood under the golden canopy of the rare giant primrose near the Alabama River bogs want to assure that ecstasy for yet another generation. And I want to believe that all of us who feel individually diminished by the loss of such beauty can reinforce our individual effectiveness by working together for some common if limited goals.

"Mankind," wrote Alfred North Whitehead not too long ago, "is in one of its rare moods of shifting outlook. The mere compulsion of tradition has lost its force. It is the business of philosophers, students, and practical men to recreate and reenact a vision of the world, conservative and radical, including those elements of reverence and order without which society lapses into riot. . . . There is now no choice before us: either we must succeed in providing a rational coordination of impulses and thoughts, or for centuries civilization will sink into a welter of minor excitements."[2]

The idea that mankind—this so human an animal—could be working at cross purposes with the natural world seems not to have been widely considered before our Vermont lawyer, scholar, and linguist published a compendious volume called *Man and Nature*. The year was 1864. Already past sixty, the author, George Perkins Marsh, was laying the groundwork for that new science now known as ecology. He spent eighteen more years studying, revising, and refining the work that he subtitled *The Earth as Modified by Human Action*. It is a book that even specialists find hard to lay down. The current edition was edited by David Lowenthal for the John Harvard Library.

Marsh notes that a maxim of the legal profession is *de minimus non curat lex*—the law is not concerned with trifles—then he adds "but in the vocabulary of nature, little and great are terms of comparison only; she knows no trifles, and her laws are as inflexible in dealing with the atom as with a continent or a planet."[3]

He recalls Babagge's "Ninth Bridgewater Treatise," which he describes as "one of the sublimest and at the same time the most fearful suggestions that have been prompted by modern science. . . ."[4] He then quotes from memory this treatise of more than a century ago:

> No atom can be disturbed in place, or undergo any change in temperature, of electrical state, or material condition without affecting, by attracting or repulsion, the surrounding atoms. These again, by the same law, transmit the influence to other atoms, and the impulse thus given tends through the whole material universe. Every human movement, every organic act, every volition, passage or emotion, every intellectual process is accompanied with atomic disturbance, and hence every such movement, every such process affects all the atoms of universal matter. Though action and reaction are equal, yet reaction does not restore disturbed atoms to their former place and condition, and the effects of the least disturbance are never cancelled. . . .[5]

Marsh adds, then, his own extension of the provocative theme in an address he wrote to a County Agricultural Association in 1847:

> There exists not alone in human conscience or in the omniscience of the Creator, but in Material Nature, an ineffaceable, imperishable record, possibly legible even to created intelligence, of every act done, every word uttered, nay every wish and purpose and thought conceived by mortal man, from the birth of our first parent to the final extinction of our race. . . .[6]

It is tantalizing to us now to recall that within the distance of an eagle's afternoon flight from Rutland, Vermont, where Marsh spoke that day, a young lady in Amherst may have been working on a brief poem, one that summed up Marsh's theme:

> A word is dead when it is said
> Some say—
>
> I say it just begins to live
> That day.[7]

Emily Dickinson was at the beginning of her poetic tasks, while Marsh was ending his astonishing careers. His law practice was closed, his discourses on language and etymology were published, his promotion of Rafn's *Icelandic Sagas* was taking much time. His competence in foreign languages enabled him to keep in touch with men of letters and science everywhere. Matthew Arnold described him as "That *rara avis*—a really well-bred and well-trained American."[8] A rare bird, indeed.

Marsh insisted on refining the book that had been his passion from his forestry and lumbering days. There were few of man's activities and their affect on the natural world that he did not tackle; he was still revising his book when he died in 1882.

"A book a century ahead of its time," scholars now say; Lewis Mumford calls it "The fountain-head of the conservation movement."[9] "Historical insight and contemporary passion make *Man and Nature* an enduring classic,"[10] in the words of its editor, and so I find it.

Although a Vermonter and man of the world gave us our first text of the vast and intricate relationship of man and his natural world, I find no evidence that he had any acquaintance with a single-minded Pennsylvania Quaker, sixty years his senior, who gave us the broadest, most enthusiastic portrait of our natural world as it appeared to those colonists of the Southeastern and Gulf Territories, halfway in time between the first records of the European explorers and our present bicentennial plans.

William Bartram gave us the naturalist's Southland—the look, the smell, the animals and plants, the hill country and the coastal bayous. He gave us, too, the intimate day-to-day happenings in the villages of the native tribes of the first Americans and records of prehistoric dwellings, artifacts, mounds, and legends. He was, even in his thirties, the first native born naturalist to qualify both as a competent scientific observer and nature artist. He abandoned school and a tradesman's apprenticeship to explore the coasts and rivers, the plains and plateaus of the Southeast territory. He was well prepared, for he had already accompanied his father, John, on explorations in the Catskills and down the eastern coast to upper Florida.

John Bartram, colonist, farmer, self-taught botanist, associate of Benjamin Franklin in public service projects, was the principal source of England's growing collection of scientific specimens and descriptions. His American born son, William, was his enthusiastic assistant. Only in this decade have William Bartram's amazing drawings become available in print. His descriptions, supplemented by these drawings and colored plates, provide a treasured record of our world as it was in the decade of our origin as a nation.

William Bartram loved the Southland. His early travels with his father had given the thirteen-year-old boy an education in plant identification and in forest lore that made possible the great tour of his life—his *Travels* (and I quote the exact title) *through North and South Carolina, Georgia, East and West Florida, and Cherokee Country, the Extensive Territories of the Muscogulges, or Creek Confederacy, and the Country of the Choctaws. Containing an Account of the Soil and Natural Productions of those Regions, together with Observations on the Manners of the Indians.* Embellished with Copper Plates. Philadelphia, 1891.

William Bartram seems to have left his father's home in Philadelphia early in 1773; he returned probably early in January 1777. He seems not to have left his Philadelphia home again. His father died in the summer of 1777, and the garden must have required much care. Then, too, preparation of the notes and journal records for publication was time consuming; the aftermath of war made publication plans difficult and financial assistance slow. Not until 1891 was the valuable manuscript finally published. In the meantime, Bartram gave help and encouragement to the naturalists who visited the garden where so many of the trees, shrubs, and herbacious plants that he and his father had collected survived. The generosity of the Bartrams allowed more ambitious scientists to copy plant descriptions, publish them, and thus be credited with their discovery. The rules of nomenclature are firm about this rule: not who finds or describes a species, but who is author of the first published description determines the name that follows the binominal designation. The Bartrams are credited with very few of the many discoveries they made.

Had the eventual publication of William's travels contained only his biological data, his scientific contribution would have been substantial, but he added to that scientific skill the fresh enthusiasm of the true explorer, whether he was describing man and the animate world or the exciting panorama and minute details of the inanimate world.

Bartram's dates may be confused, his measurements may falter, but his descriptions are in proper Latin, as the new Linnean system required. Four of those species discovered and described for the first time William found in the Taensa (Tensaw) area of what is now Baldwin County in Alabama. The type localities, as the recorded discovery sites are called, are not protected, although some of the species are not widely distributed nor well known.

One of the Bartram discoveries, a flowering tree from the coastal area of Georgia, has not been found again in the wild since 1803. Had the Bartrams not preserved the species and propagated it, the world might have doubted its validity. It is referred to as the lost Franklinia, named for Benjamin Franklin, a friend of the Bartrams. Many other Southern species maintain a precarious foothold in the face of rapid and massive changes.

For one of those species Bartram reserved the most exuberant description of his entire publication. That plant was the giant golden primrose, close relative of the ubiquitous *Oenothera biennis* included in the agricultural weed list of many states. The giant primrose, *Oenothera grandiflora,* attracted to Alabama in September 1912 an expedition of plant scientists from the most famous botanical centers of New England, who joined one of the most renowned of all plant scientists, Hugo De Vries, the Dutch geneticist who had based his theory of mutations upon experiments with primroses of the genus *Oenothera.*

The New York Botanical Society initiated the plan to bring De Vries to the Bartram site in Alabama and instructed a Dr.

Tracey of Biloxi, Mississippi, to search the Taensa area to make certain the rare flower was there. He did so and mailed a post card from Taensa with three words, "I have it." In the New York office, when the card from Dr. Tracy arrived, was Dr. Roland Harper, that salty, indefatigable, lovable botanist who for more than half a century was connected with The University of Alabama. He saw to it that the students, faculty, and townspeople of Tuscaloosa were invited to hear De Vries before the party left by train for Mobile and then by boat up river to the site landing. Dr. Harper and a biology instructor left the train at Jackson and traveled by horsecart across the Alabama river and bottom lands to the landing. The rain never ceased, but they met the scientists the next day at Dixie Landing, where they found the famous plant. Periodically the rare primrose is rediscovered, much to the amusement of local residents who wonder, now, how to keep it growing in those wasteplaces that are being changed into front lawns, fishing camps, and industrial sites.

The fortuitous circumstance of Bartram's visit to Alabama the very year of our nation's independence prompted us early in the 1950's to propose that we identify Bartram's trail in Alabama. When the National Trails Act was passed in 1968, it seemed reasonable to hope that a Bartram trail could become an interstate effort.

Proposals are inexpensive, but implementation is difficult to achieve. The National Trails Council, an outgrowth of a national administration effort to further trails development, has twice recommended that the Bartram trail be designated for bicentennial observance. Georgia and Florida have joined Alabama in asking Congress to authorize a feasibility study preparatory to naming the Bartram route as a National Scenic and Historic Trail. Development of the Bartram Trail would enable all the Southeastern and Gulf states to join in a bicentennial effort that would celebrate two historical events and would establish the country's first interstate coastal and lowland trail. Eventually it could extend from Philadelphia to Louisiana, touching every coastal state and including both water and hiking routes. The natural features, the species and habitats that could thus be preserved, include some rarities that might otherwise disappear in the present decade.

Preserving art and artifacts, saving old structures and furnishings, all of these efforts are important. But there is value, I think, in using our past to save our future, not bargaining away our future while we dwell on our past achievements. History lives if we protect and enjoy the landscape the explorers found, just as it lives in the artifacts they built.

Bartram's sites and discoveries are important, but there were other discoverers and there are other famous sites to be noted. Fort Toulouse at the juncture of the two great rivers Coosa and Tallapoosa, which form the Alabama, was described by many early visitors. Bartram recorded some of the exciting events of his visit there in December of 1775. But the most notable scientist to visit and describe the geology of the Alabama River was that eminent father of stratigraphic geology Sir Charles Lyell. Sir Charles and Mrs. Lyell made the trip by river boat in 1846, having traveled by train from Cheaha to Montgomery. Not only did they make the trip downstream from Montgomery to Mobile, collecting geological specimens and fossils whenever the boat picked up or dropped cargo, but they came by boat up the Tombigbee and Warrior Rivers to The University of Alabama campus. The journey in flood time made it look, Lyell wrote, as if the forests grew in a vast lake; they had to wait until the floods subsided to see the falls at Tuscaloosa, which appeared to be only rapids in higher water. Lyell's journey into the coal fields and his comments about the similarity of the fossils of the coal measures to those of Europe are well known. But the impact of his entire visit, the sites he described, and the restrained, perceptive comments about social and political problems are part of the history we could well recover.

If tourism is to have meaning beyond the carpark, restaurant, and swimming pool, we might well capitalize on the writings of these guests who cared about the people and places they visited. Lyell took deep interest in the absentee ownership he felt was

so destructive in much of the area he visited. He and Mrs.
Lyell went to Rooke's Valley and regretted that the self-taught
black linguist they met there was being sent to Liberia to teach
Greek and Latin instead of teaching in Alabama.

Both the Lyells viewed the stars they could not see from their
more northerly home through a telescope set up by a Dr. Barnard.
They noted with satisfaction that the lens was shipped from
England. Where, one wonders, is that telescope?

Lyell's visit is a fine peg on which to hang some natural
history site preservation. Lyell's descriptions of both the Tuscaloosa area and the Alabama River are worth noting. The Clai-
borne site, particularly, has more than once been proposed for
preservation. So far, support for some method of insuring its
protection eludes us. But, unless scientists and historians join
hands with conservationists and those versed in the arts and
humanities, these places will be lost.

Much remains to be told, in the way of natural history records,
but I shall conclude with a small gem of literary and scientific
value—Philip Gosse's *Letters from Alabama,* published in England in 1859.

Gosse, a young Englishman, came by boat to Mobile, then
traveled by river boat to King's Landing, not far from Selma, to
teach in a small private school for the better part of a year. His
scientific training was in entomolgy, though he seems to have
been as well acquainted with the rest of the animal and plant
world as with insects. Indeed there was little he did not recognize
—vegetable, animal, or mineral. His precise, clean prose is packed
with natural history. He was careful regarding generalities about
social problems; still, like the Lyells, he intimates that problems
stemming from the racial issue could not long be deferred.

Philip Henry Gosse, out in the woods during November in 1856,
found the large-flowered evening primrose *Oenothera grandiflora*
that Bartram had described from Alabama almost a century earlier,
"with its fine blossoms of brilliant yellow—as wide as a tea-
cup."[11] To his delight he saw a flock of the now extinct Carolina
parakeets as he drove to Selma. He likened them to "an immense

shawl of green satin on which an irregular pattern was worked in scarlet and gold and azure."[12] Gosse left Alabama as the snow-birds (juncos) arrived; he regretted not seeing the entire pageant of the bird's migration and was sickened by the young boys' sport of carrying lighted pine knots into the woods and attacking resting birds with clubs. "Le jeu," he said, "ne vaut pas le chandell."[13] Truly, much that we do, I fear, is not worth the candle. Today's students of English literature may not know that the early twentieth-century English editor Sir Edmund Gosse had a father who once described in detail a bit of the Alabama landscape.

Perhaps it is presumptious to make even so modest a proposal as I suggest, but as a member for many years of the Alabama Academy of Science I believe it is time to urge the entire scientific community to join with historical and conservation societies and the councils of the arts and the humanities to identify those sites that can now be withdrawn from development without severe planning shifts or economic loss and preserve them as a heritage of lasting value.

A recent *Journal of the Alabama Academy of Science* describes another endangered habitat, a site of *Neviusia,* a rare Alabama shrub first described from Tuscaloosa. One of the few natural sites for this plant and associated species in northeast Alabama is threatened simply by the widening of a highway. The authors of the report are deeply concerned. "Just a little consultation would have saved it,"[14] they said. A little consultation. Even within the walls of a single institution, sometimes we do not speak much to each other. Consultation implies mutual understanding. It might not be too difficult once a small start has been made.

Alabama scientists and conservationists have joined to study and consult about the status of the state's endangered vertebrates. The report has been published, and it is clear that some of the endangered species have overlapping territories. Some would overlap, also, the crucial botanical habitats that need to be saved. There are the dwindling pitcher plant bogs of South Alabama and the sand dunes with their greatly endangered biological communities. But one cannot save a bog or a dune without preserving a buffer zone, sometimes of considerable extent.

The proposed Sipsey Wilderness with its transitional animal and plant life, is so near to being saved that one can scarcely await finality. The Taensa with the Bartram type localities, the Central Alabama sites of the Alabama *Croton* and *Neviusea* associations, the river bluff sites with geological exposures, all are in need of our care. Only scientists and alert site planners, together with a perceptive and enlightened public, can accomplish these remnant recoveries.

Focus for such areas excites the imagination. What of a Mohr Museum in tribute to the pioneer author of *Plant Life of Alabama?* What of an outdoor center or a series of centers in tribute to Eugene V. Smith, who brought distinguished scientists to Alabama and who supervised publication of many volumes? What of a Harper Path, a simple walkway around the perimeter of this state that Roland Harper made his home? And why not a Blanche Dean Nature Garden? The working heroes and heroines are many, the tributes all too few. Legal procedures are available, others could be enacted; even now available funds are not being used. The prestige of the universities and the scientific community might turn the tide.

Alabama is one of a very few states with no protected holdings such as are provided by the Nature Conservancy. Recently, as an example, more than 200,000 acres south of Albuquerque, New Mexico, including historic villages and natural areas, were given protected status. Such recoveries of valuable natural and historic resources cannot be accomplished by armchair travelers nor by placards. For this kind of retrieval we must rely on scientists for technical data, on historians, artists, and conservationists for evaluation, and on an alert and awakened public for financial support.

You may have studied, as I did, a famous essay called *The American Scholar*. George Perkins Marsh also wrote an essay with this title and delivered it at the Phi Beta Kappa lecture at Cambridge in 1847. "The American scholar," he said, is not a recluse devoted to quiet research, but one who lives and acts in the busy whirl of the great world, shares the anxieties and the hazards of commerce, the toils and rivalries of the learned professions, or the fierce strife of contending political factions, or who is engaged perhaps in some industrial pursuit, and is oftener stunned by the clang of the forge and the hum of machinery, than refreshed by the voice of the Muse."[15]

It was this same man of many interests who wrote "Sight is a faculty, seeing is an art."[16] It will require both sight and seeing if we are to save the fragile, threatened landscapes of the South.

NOTES

[1]George Perkins Marsh, *Man and Nature,* ed. David Lowenthal (Cambridge, Mass.: The Belknap Press of Harvard Univ. Press, 1965), p. xvii.

[2]Wallace B. Donham, *Business Adrift* (New York: McGraw-Hill, 1931), p. xxix. In introduction by Alfred North Whitehead .

[3]Marsh, p. 464.

[4]Ibid., n. 35.

[5]Ibid.

[6]It is probably this speech that was quoted in the *Christian Examiner,* 68 (1860), 41.

[7]*The Poems of Emily Dickinson,* ed. Thomas H. Johnson (Cambridge: Harvard Univ. Press, 1955). Poem 1212, 3rd version.

[8]Matthew Arnold to Frances Arnold, June 22, 1865, in *Letters of Matthew Arnold 1848-1888,* I (New York, 1895), 329.

[9]Lewis Mumford, *The Brown Decades: A Study of the Arts in America, 1865-1895* (New York, 1931), p. 78.

[10]Marsh, pp. ix, x.

[11]Philip Henry Gosse, FRS, *Letters From Alabama* (N.A.) *Chiefly Relating to Natural History* (London: Morgan and Chase, Tichborne, 280, High Holborn, 1859), p. 292.

[12]Ibid., p. 298.

[13]Ibid., p. 297.

[14]*Journal of the Alabama Academy of Science.*

[15]"Human Knowledge: A Discourse Delivered before the Massachusetts Alpha of the Phi Beta Kappa Society, at Cambridge, August 26, 1847" (Boston, 1847), p. 4. Also in Marsh, p. xxvi.

[16]Marsh, p. 15.

The South is Rising Again— In Living Colors

TOM GILMORE

TOM GILMORE—Tom Gilmore was born on May 1, 1941, in Forkland, Alabama, in rural Greene County. After graduating from the Greene County Training School (now called Paramount High School), Gilmore attended Selma University Junior College and lived briefly in California. He returned to his home county in 1964 and took an active role in the civil rights movement as it was being organized and let in Alabama by The Reverend Jesse Jackson and the late Dr. Martin Luther King, Jr. After one unsuccessful attempt at the office, Gilmore was elected sheriff of Greene County in 1970. He was reelected in 1974.

Reflecting a little bit on the history of the mid-1860's, I suspect that the young men who fought in the war in the Southland must have created in their minds the slogan: The South is going to rise again. And through many years of being occupied by Federal troops, their economy smashed, and facing the whole problem of putting the South back together again, they must have kept that dream: The South is going to rise again. However, I doubt very seriously that they thought that the South would rise again in living colors—black and white.

So, if I have any prejudices, if I have any hangups, positive hangups, it is the Southland, the Southern part of the United States of America, and more particularly the rural Southland —probably because I was born there in Greene County, Alabama, and you can't hardly get any more rural than Greene County. But more than that, even though there was prevalent in Greene County a bad kind of relationship, the master-servant type relationship, that I certainly didn't enjoy, that I don't think is

50

healthy for any group of individuals, it was better than the non-existent relationship in the Northland, and I think that master-slave relationship can be, and has been, and is being changed, and not only in some sections of the southern part of this country, into a man to man kind of relationship where whites and blacks as individuals respect each other more. I think Greene County today is the best example of the victory of the civil rights movement in the Southland; it has probably had more impact than the Selma-Montgomery march. I know that most of you have read and heard about the Selma-Montgomery march, and I know that you all understand that it was probably the thing that forced that civil rights bill through the legislature and on past the president's pen, but Greene County represents the new phase of the civil rights movement. It is the result of the work of Dr. King and the men of the Southern Christian Leadership Conference of that day and the Student Non-violent Coordinating Committee, since they were the most active in that neck of the woods at that time. Greene County clearly points up that if people are willing to struggle and willing to fight, not just for days, but for months and years, that which one would think would be unobtainable can come. Greene County's victory is unique in that no other county and no other movement and no other group of people have produced in the Southland the kind of results that we have in Greene County —political results. And the one thing that is probably most unique is that almost overnight there was a complete change of government, that of the conservative, racist whites keeling over into the hands of black liberals, who had been, for the most part, deeply involved in the civil rights movement. Judge Branch, who is the only black probate judge in the Southland, had been the local NAACP leader in the community since 1962 and was also the president of the Civic Organization. I was involved in a suit in the early 1960's. We thought that we couldn't get much justice in Greene County, so we decided that we would personally make up a jury system and go into court and ask the court to correct the problems that we were having with the jury system. And, you know, when you get into court things kind of linger along a little while and the pressures start coming. At that point, I decided to leave. I may have been running away; I don't know.

I had heard that young men should go West, and I heard that it was a good place, especially for young black men. But I had my disappointments in Los Angeles, California. I saw blatant and obvious racism there. I saw hate equal to that I had seen in Alabama. I saw problems with the schools like those in Alabama. The very first time that I was called "nigger" by a police officer was in Los Angeles. So I decided that it was about time for me to come back home where I was born, and I decided that if I was going to stop people from calling me "nigger" I might as well stop people in the Southland from calling me "nigger." So, I got involved in the civil rights movement.

I had planned to do it just for a vacation, you know, like some of the younger people did, just for a year or so—get in, get out, then go back, probably to New York through Philadelphia. But it was no vacation I had. I was called "nigger" for the first time by an Alabama state trooper. He accused me of coming from California to start trouble in Selma because I had a California license plate on my automobile. So, even though I had planned to start something, but not in Selma, I decided I would go ahead to Selma the next weekend. During this time the heat of the movement was on in Selma, Alabama, and I must say that I got caught up in the spirit with the message that Dr. King preached. Dr. King gave me some hope through his message that all men could be free and that freedom, justice, and equality are great, are worth your working for, are worth your giving your life for. So, you see, the Greene County system, power structure, changed from a conservative, racist type system over to a black system that was especially sensitive to the kind of problems that we were faced with at that time. We would like at this time to believe that Greene County offers more hope than any other place in the nation as far as racial harmony is concerned, and economic growth, and just a better general social condition. And I do not think we can overstress racial harmony.

All of us know that our nation is in trouble now, and recession and inflation are the big talk now, and Watergate is big talk, and some of the political leaders are going to jail, and some are waiting for a few months to go to jail. We have our troubles, but still and all racism is the big problem in this country. Our nation is experiencing a kind of division that is heading us toward separate black and white societies. This has been costly. It has cost millions of dollars in property destruction; it has cost us many human lives. God only knows how much anger and hostility people still hold within themselves because of what has gone on in the past few years. But if we cannot bring this trend to a halt, we can rest assured that we have death, hell, and destruction waiting for us at the end.

In Greene County, and I don't want to sell Greene County as some type of Utopia and urge everybody to, all of a sudden, sell and rent and give up whatever he has and come on to Greene County, we have our problems. We have our problems as you have your problems here in Tuscaloosa. We have our problems as you have your problems here in the university community. Our problems are many, but we have made progress. We have done something. And when you have done something, you will have progress.

We sometimes run into situations that prohibit us from doing things that we know need to be done. For example, we had a situation in which the commissioners and the judge decided, in good faith, that they would arrange for better ambulance services for the community. They decided that they would contract with the Demopolis Police Department and make sure that everybody would be served. After they did this, somebody discovered that they had no legal authority to do it. There is no law that would enable the commissioners to approve spending public funds in this way, and, even though these men were looking out for the interests of their community, their hand got called. The auditors came in and said, "this is an incorrect expenditure and you're going to have to replace this money," and, of course, the press came in and wrote a story that implied that these gentlemen were mishandling funds, more or less omitting the fact that these gentlemen were trying to do good for their community. And, of course, they didn't leave me out on that trip.

I had gone to California to the National Convention of the Sheriff's Association (I had a better time in California this time than before), and they accused the county of having helped me along on that trip. They also said that I couldn't have *Jet* and *Ebony* magazines in my office at the expense of the county. (Of course, they didn't bother to stop me from getting *Field and Stream*.)

We have an antiquated state law that needs revising and that causes all kind of problems. I have a problem in feeding prisoners. I am only authorized to spend one dollar and twenty-five cents per day on prisoners' food. I have to provide food for my prisoners with a buck-twenty-five per day! (Of course, when I was elected sheriff it was ninty cents a day per prisoner.) So, we are limited by law in what we can do. So I don't want to say that Greene County, Alabama, is a problem free area, but we are coming into the home-stretch. I do want to convey that we are a group of hard working people, and we realize that we have problems, but we are working towards solving those problems.

Greene County, as you know, is among the poorest in this nation. It is probably about the fifth poorest county nationwide and, in the sixties, seventy-five percent of our housing was sub-standard. Our educational system has had little concern about meeting the educational needs of the students of Greene County. But we are moving ahead.

Unemployment is one of our greatest problems in Greene County right now. We are trying to encourage industry to come to our town, but it is not easy. Industry takes a look at counties with predominately black populations, and they have all kinds of worries about whether the community's politics and government are going to be stable. They do complicated studies to find out that they cannot come in to help provide employment for our people.

Another issue that people got more excited about back in the sixties was education. For the first time, folks in Greene County, watching television and listening to the radio, became aware of what was going on in the world around them, especially in terms of education and the *Brown v. Board of Education* case in Topeka, Kansas. Blacks saw education as the hope, and they saw a real hope to get that education.

But, to digress for a moment, let me say that blacks have always felt that their best hope lay in getting an education and in making sure that their children got an education. As soon as Abraham Lincoln signed the Emancipation Proclamation and as soon as black folk really got free in places like South Carolina, the first thing they did was to start building schools, building schools with their own hands, because they knew that after feeding their children, this was the most important thing they could do for them.

And, of course, several religious groups have been involved with helping black folks get an education. The Quakers were involved way back during and after the Civil War, and they helped us in Greene County in the sixties. Education, then, has been very important to black people from the time of Booker T. Washington, to the time of the Brown decision, to this day. It may strike different kinds of fear in the hearts of some people in the white community, but we cannot settle for a poor education, for our children's education is their best hope for the future.

In 1955 Dr. King and the Montgomery boycott became household words, so people were beginning to feel what was going on around them. And then soon after that was Anniston, Alabama, where a few folks were trying to get to Montgomery or into Mississippi on the freedom ride and the bus was burned. And then there were all the things that went on in Danville, Virginia, and Greensboro, North Carolina, and the sit-ins, and the bloody trail of the freedom riders, who were beaten at most of the stops they made as they tried to get to the Southland. Birmingham, of course, in '63 was a costly operation—young girls were killed in the 16th Street Baptist Church. And then after that Selma. Selma became the place where we realized that politics was the way to correct the situation in the South. The nation is political, so let's get political, too. Let's make sure that everyone has the right to vote. Then demonstrations started in Greensboro, Alabama; Demopolis, Alabama; Aliceville, Alabama; Eutaw, Alabama. I had the responsibility of leading some of those demonstrations, and it was really a new awakening for me. I think if I have ever had a real religious experience or a real heart-warming experience it was my stay in the civil rights movement and in particular my involvement in direct action. When I had an opportunity to meet face-to-face with those gentlemen that I had feared most of my life, with those gentlemen that I had learned to hate, and I was able to keep myself in check and discipline myself, I found that disciplining myself had a lot to do with disciplining others. However, it failed on a couple of occasions, and I ended up getting beat up in the district attorney's office by the former sheriff. It was a terrible beating, for I had decided that I was going to be nonviolent at that particular time. There were a couple of young ladies who were part of that demonstration—a sit-in in the district attorney's office—and when the sheriff came in and asked why we were there and what we wanted, before we could tell him he was beating on us, and one of the girls was struck; immediately I became angry at the force that he used to strike her, and I went, as I have been trained to do, over to use my body to protect the young lady, and, of course, I sustained about five or six big blows from a walking stick. Then my anger left and I decided that it was my responsibility at that point to get in charge of the situation, and I remember, even though the sheriff was doing a very good job of swinging his stick, I remember the moment when I stayed there and protected everyone to make sure that everyone was out of the door. I decided that I would work against him in his next election—not as the candidate for sheriff; I had no idea at all that I would want that responsibility. As a matter of fact, when I was selected I was over in Chicago with the civil rights movement having an evening of fun; when I was called, I thought the person was making a joke. But the hostility, the anger, the violence that we saw and experienced in Greene County did not turn us around, did not make us too angry to take our eyes off the goal. We saw hate, we saw fear, and we saw it spread like wildfire. We saw men leave their jobs and come to the school to block people from coming in, with a stand not any different from the stand that Governor Wallace took at The University of Alabama. We found that if we would be persistent, if we would be courageous, if we would be untiring in our efforts then surely we would be able to overcome and gain a political base in Greene County. Greene County is real, it is moving, it is working, it represents, as I said earlier, the new phase of the movement. Dr. King talked long ago about black and white children going to school together and sons of slaves and sons of slave owners sitting down at the table together to work out their problems, and we are experiencing a bit of that. We know that there are those, both black and white, who have their own self-interests at heart and who will do whatever to make the thing go the way they want it to go. We are aware that we have got racists, both black and white, who are trying to make the system go their way. We have got untiring efforts on the part of whites to try to make sure that the system comes back like it was fifteen years ago. There are blacks who are trying to make the system work for blacks only.

But the majority of the people of Greene County want to see a system that will provide good government in Greene County, Alabama. They want to see free and open politics so that whoever would like to can get involved. They want to see a situation where all of the people can feel this way, not just blacks and not just whites.

In the country nowadays, we see very, very little similar to the Greene County situation. Surely in Atlanta I suspect that Congressman Andrew Young represents pleasant hopes for his district. He represents the thing that the civil rights movement can encourage its followers to be involved with. Across the country we find that one of the main problems is that we had too little participation by blacks and other ethnic groups in our political process. In this country we only have a half dozen sheriffs out of more than 3,000 counties, and four of those sheriffs are in Alabama. One other sheriff is in Michigan and one is in Camden,

New Jersey. There is only one black probate judge, very few black superintendents of education, and very, very, very few black chiefs of police in office in this country. If we are going to have a system that will hold on for us and that will hold on for our children and our children's children, we have got to dedicate ourselves to making sure that we are going to get racism out of that system; we must open the system so that everyone can feel free to function; we must make sure that everybody is protected under the laws of our Constitution. We must remember that if anybody's rights can be abused because of his race, or his religion, or his sex, or his nationality, all of our rights are in jeopardy. Yesterday they hanged us because we were black; today they hang us because we protest; tomorrow they may hang you because you do not think like they think. I am involved in law enforcement as sheriff of Greene County, Alabama, and, of course, when you look across the nation you find that blacks and other ethnic groups are complaining that police use no discretion, that the police are brutal in almost every case when they deal with them, that the police will overreact, and that the police represent the society of the economic elite—a very small group of millionaires. But I suggest to you that we can take a look at Greene County, a serious look at Greene County. However small it is, I think it can be of some national significance. It is important to the country to see that the people in Greene County can work together and have a good society, a sane society. In four years, neither the sheriff's office nor any other law enforcement officer down in that county has had any reason to shoot anybody. Maybe in other jurisdictions, where the law enforcement officers do feel it necessary to shoot a few people each year, those shootings ought to be investigated. When you look at Greene County and see that the government can work for all of the people down there and that folks can feel free to protest, then we can apply that to our system in this nation. It is our responsibiliy to make the system work for us, and our children, and our children's children.

Mayflies No More:
A Fresh Look at
the Southern Woman

PAT DERIAN

PATRICIA M. DERIAN—Patricia M. Derian, Democratic National Committeewoman from Mississippi and member of the National Board of Directors of the American Civil Liberties Union, has been active throughout the 1960's and 1970's in the fight for human rights. Derian has served on the Board of Directors of the *Ms.* Magazine Foundation, and this present paper is concerned largely with the present status of the Southern woman. Derian's interests, however, extend into many fields: politics, mental health, and civil liberties of all kinds.

Derian has been deeply involved in the decision-making apparatus of the Democratic party. She has served as a member of the Democratic Policy Council and its Executive Committee, the Credentials Committee, and the Charter Commission. She was a delegate to the Democratic national conventions of 1968 and 1972 and was vice-chairman of the important Rules Committee of the 1972 Democratic convention.

A graduate of the University of Virginia School of Nursing, Derian has a continuing interest in community and mental health. She has been a board member of the Family Service Association and the Mississippi Mental Health Association, and she is a past member of the Academy of Religion and Mental Health. Derian has served as chairman of the Southern Regional Council Task Force on Health.

Derian's commitment to equal justice has been demonstrated by active participation in various branches of the American Civil Liberties Union. She is on the Board of Directors of the Mississippi ACLU, the National Board of Directors of the ACLU, and she is a member of the Board of Directors of the Center for Correctional Justice in Washington, D.C. At present she is an active member of the Mississippi Equal Rights Amendment Ratification Council.

Southern women—what a problem we have been. Panting in the

59

bushes, fanning ourselves on our pedestals, or steaming in each other's kitchens, we have kept our region hopping and the fantasies and imaginations of generations of other Americans (writers, moralists, and Miss America officials among them) gasping in mesmerized wonder.

Utter the two words in any gathering. Everyone is ready to describe her. Assign a class to write an essay on Southern women. Would any hand go up to ask, "Which Southern women?" No, all would set to work with certainty and vigor. They know who we are.

Absentmindedly, we reinforce the myth. Whether it is, "Who, little old me?" with a flutter of lashes or, "Lord, honey, don't give me that stuff," we confirm. We can use it to gain cover to pursue our own course, but do we know it? Do we have a common course?

We have the stereotypes.

When people speak of Southern women they generally mean white women—white, middleclass women. Girls, matrons, and old ladies with destinies as certain as the mayfly's. (The mayfly is an insect of the order of epheoptera having delicate, membranous wings with the front pair much larger than the rear.) They spring into being at seventeen as respectable Chi O's and Tri Delts, wrestling around on the third tee of every country club south of Maryland. They shimmer, pout, dance in rows, march at the front of bands, diet, make B's without any brains, sometimes if plied with whiskey submit, and always marry. They teach school until the babies come, belong to the Junior Auxiliary, a name brand church, stuff their children with rules and cheese grits until they are forty. At forty they garden, play bridge, fall to drink, and bore their husbands to death. Upon achieving widowhood they travel around the world looking at castles, great gardens, art treasures, and needlework through the ages. They worry their children, work on the grandchildren, and guard our way of life. They are well dressed, very tidy, and anti-intellectual throughout. They always make certain that they are treated with proper respect, because they are white and not dirt poor.

That is part of the myth. Yet, we know her. She is here among us, one of us, our sister. How did she get that way? Ask either of our Southern Lillians—Smith or Hellman. Ask Eudora Welty or Tennessee Williams. But don't ask Faulkner—he bought that lady. If you hold her individually responsible for her life, it is necessary to concede that she gave over to the societal expectation. Maybe because she never discovered that there was a choice. Maybe because she would not have to wash dishes or walk the baby or suffer a frown from authority. But in a life surrounded by rules, one seldom hears an idea. Hold her responsible then, for she has worked much mischief, yet, understand that there are mitigating circumstances.

We have the angel. How the blood has run in her name. Our mayfly clambered upon the pedestal and dared anyone to knock her down; the angel was too ethereal to notice. Lillian Smith said, "All a woman can expect from lingering on exalted heights is a bad chill afterward" (*Killers of the Dream,* 1961). Our history is peppered with women who were either born to the perch or scaled it later, who hopped off once they noticed where they were.

Aloft, the angel stands for motherhood, God, culture, and her own utter defenselessness, except in time of war, pestilence, flood, or famine when she works, day and night, like a dog. White men, individually and collectively, have shot, maimed, lynched, and imprisoned black men for her. Black men could not resist her body due to its utter desirability and the probable, uncontrollable black instincts. This was hard work for the white men but quite lucrative. They were rewarded for her defense with all the political power, cheap labor, and relief from the necessity of providing adequate educational and civic services to the black community. In her name, we dehumanized our black kin.

She was the virgin mother of our own fractious children, evil and guilt. The original sin of the white South is fully as handicapping as the Christian notion of it. We are enervated by its inevitability; it is too much to cope with in all this heat. The angel was pure myth, though the out-of-the-way position was not. Only a handful of women ever believed in her; everyone else pretended, for one reason or another.

This generation's beauty queens are mayflies. It is the memory of last generation's beauty queens that still nourishes the myth of the wanton, poor white beauty rolling in the canebrake, in a frenzy of primal excitement, right up to the day she packs her ragged dresses and trudges up the dirt road to fame and fortune as a national sex goddess. If she fails, she is the mindless, easy going, small town prostitute who gives pleasure till she is thirty, when all of her teeth fall out and her body shrivels or balloons. She goes at once to a shack in the country, produces fourteen children and pulls the family plow. If she succeeds, she realizes as her beauty fades that it was not enough and commits suicide or goes to live in Spain.

Then there is the plain, Southern churchwoman: Baptist, Presbyterian, or Methodist. She is the one with the pursed mouth, the only one who wears glasses and is, of course, frigid. Life's pleasure is the denunciation of evil. Her evil includes drinking whiskey, integration of the races, sass in children, long-haired boys, and talking dirty. She feeds her family, makes sure they are clean, protects them from communism as a member of the P.T.A., and is coming around on the question of girl's basketball. If she has an embarrassingly big bosom, she wishes she didn't and sleeps in her bra. Her church circle sustains her from thirty-eight to the grave. Before thirty-eight she was a mother or a daughter.

So much for the Southern white female stereotypes. There are others, but they are variations of the broad general categories. Eighty percent of Southern women are white. And the ready generalization is that they are all as useless as weeds.

If the whites are the weeds, the Southern black woman is the fruit-bearing tree, sturdy, lush, comforting, nourishing, and well rooted. She has served us all—men, women, and children, black and white—as matriarch, mammy, auntie, field worker, phoenix, and Florabel. She has been the enduring witness, rising from every adversity intact, wise and good, motherly, but superficially sexless.

Tempering justice with mercy while making beaten biscuits, she ran the white household with a velvet glove and her own with an iron fist. It is said that she loved her white children as well as she loved her own. It is certain that she saw more of the former, since she worked twelve hours a day. And they surely looked nicer than her own, since they did not live on four or five dollars a week or wear hand-me-downs from Mammy's family. You can see her yet on the Aunt Jemima box, plump and smiling.

She did have some disagreeable habits: dipping snuff, going barefooted, and parading a series of mysterious "husbands" before the children. However, every white knew that Negroes did not have the same standards. Some white writers and moralists worried that two coexisting moral codes would surely lead to the corruption of the finer by the baser. But most whites found it quite amusing since the "antics" of black people offered the only opportunity to talk about sex at all. If you had had to rely on the spoken word, you would know that people died and were born, but you would never suspect that white people had anything personally to do with sex.

While Mammy is still on the tip of memory, she lives only in literature today. Mammy was the Southern black woman and entirely estimable.

The Southern black girl was someone else entirely. Black girlhood lasted from puberty till death. There was no telling what a black girl might do. High stepping and lusty, she was always ready for a tumble, anywhere, which was engaging and convenient. The drawback was that in idle moments she would just as soon seduce an innocent little white boy, any preacher, or, if the fancy struck her, a fine, upstanding white husband. She would drop a baby like a fish drops eggs, steal anything she wanted, and spit in the soup if you didn't keep an eye on her. And she did cause trouble. Why, she would as soon pull a knife as look at you, cut a woman out of jealousy and a man out of sheer bad temper. She was the serpent in this garden and a mighty pretty little thing. She is gone, too.

There are few current myhts about black women. A new one is being constructed, but it has not been given wide credence yet.

This is the cool, tough, sharp-tongued calculator who may use a man or put him down. She is beginning to turn up in the movies as a sexy woman of high achievement and ability completely without tenderness. And Superfly is her friend. They are equals and work together.

An interesting consequence of the civil rights movement is the examination of the images of black people as imposed by whites. There has been a great cultural weighing of values, an assessment of how black people think they are and want to be. In the course of this scrutiny, black women are giving attention to the picture of themselves as castrating matriarchs. Mammy might have been a pillar of comfort to whites, but to blacks, she drove her man out, forced her children to suppress their wit, brains, and ambition. She gave her best to the whites and her meanest to her own, reducing black men to lonely despair and her children to zombies. In order for a stereotype to mean anything, people have to pay homage to it. With guilt or pride the stereotyped too, must acquiesce. Today's black woman refuses to succumb; on the contrary, she is actively at work to destroy every vestige of it. At first glance the growing image of the tough, competent woman seems to be a variation on the old model. But there is a very real difference—she is projecting her equal footing, her determination to work with men. There is unity on the rejection of the matriarch. But, it is at this point that a debate is engaged. Should black women step back and push black men forward, to compensate for the powerless past they have endured? Or should they go along together? The discussion will probably go on for years with some women going one way and other another. The immediate lesson for all women is that they can escape the myth and refuse to be bound by it simply by saying no.

The myths were made by men and treasured by many women. An Ohio physiologist told me that she was past thirty before she stopped wishing she had been born a Southern woman and then only because she had finally acknowledged that she was never going to be one. California's golden girl, always described anatomically, has disappeared. Feminists, women's libbers, and

"Ms. Magnolia," to one Mississippi editor, may supplant us in the conventional wisdom, relieve us of our anachronistic burdens. I had a letter from an architect recently. She said, "Remember, all the vestal virgins got was a porch to hold up with their heads." The porch is not even the main part of the building. And that is what the make-believe has cost us: whether we are the decorative pillars or the objects on the pedestal, we are removed from the public life and decision making of the society.

Ada Esser says that mythmaking happens on the frontiers of experience, making the unknown manageable, useful, and less frightening and is a group experience that men have always had. Women's group experience has been in service; as my friend the architect says, "Keeping the pot boiling is hardly the kind of group experience myths are made of—not exactly an Apollo team effort." And that may be another reason women are calling for change: they have heard all the old myth stories, want some new ones, and are willing to go out and make their own.

What are Southern women doing? There are twenty-four million Southern females fourteen years old and over. Forty percent over sixteen work. Forty percent of the fifteen million married women work: 33 per cent of them have children under six, and 48 percent have children six to seventeen. About 31 percent do clerical work, another 15 percent do professional or technical work.

About half of the white women have more than eleven years and nine months of school. For black women, nine years is the median. Only about eight percent of Southern women have had four or more years of college. The woman who researched these figures looked in her category to see how she was doing. With five or more years of collgee, there were 5,239 other white women in her middle-aged bracket making over $15,000 a year. She found six hundred and thirty-five black women with four or more years of college who worked full-time in 1969 as private household workers with median wages of $2,143.

Among all women working full-time between the ages of twenty-five and sixty-five in 1969, white women had a median income of $4,621, and black women had a median of $2,973. Even those who had five or more years of college only had a median of $8,411. One thing a lot of Southern women are doing is working, and they are not getting rich doing it.

Seven hundred and sixty thousand Southern families are headed by women who are poor (U.S. Sliding Scale of Poverty) and four-fifths of them have children. Three hundred and eighty thousand of these poor women have children under six; almost half of them are in the labor force. Sixty-three percent of the black female-headed families are poor compared to thirty-five percent of the white female-headed families. When the next figures come out, we will see how many of these working women are right at the minimum wage of two dollars an hour and what, if any, difference it has made in the median incomes. The new wage and hour legislation has brought a lot of people, previously not covered by the minimum wage, under its provisions.

Eighty percent of Southern women have been or are married; for the most part they have children, and those that work do so because they need the money. Since under ten percent have completed college, more than three-fourths of them work at jobs that pay well under $10,000 a year.

Last week I called around, asking career workers—executives, bank officers, and women in high positions—if they were paid as much as men doing the same job. With the exception of federal employees, the answer was no. The employers I questioned explained that men were heads of households, had heavier responsibilities, could stay late at night, and were more oriented to moving ahead than women. They believed to a man that a woman who had worked fifteen or twenty years might walk out at any moment, leaving them high and dry, if they had invested any advanced training or money in her. A few years ago, I was standing on a sidewalk in mid-August in Jackson, Mississippi, with a corporation president who described a very high paying, short-term job, which he offered to me with the selling point that I might want to pick up enough money to earn a mink coat. I wasn't cold so we weren't able to do business.

Illustrations of unrealistic thinking only hint at the overall assumption that Southern women are cupcakes willing to pay anything to keep men opening doors for them and lighting their cigarettes because that is what makes them happy. A lot of women agree with the idea that there is a trade involved. In order to be paid on the basis of experience, ability, and work, in order to make decisions about your own life, you will have to sacrifice common courtesies. That is rank nonsense, and Southern women are coming to see it for what it is.

In 1971 and 1972, Louis Harris conducted polls on American women's opinions for the Virginia Slims cigarette people. In the first poll, 39 percent of Southern women favored efforts to strengthen or change women's status in society, 41 per cent were opposed and 20 percent did not know how they felt. In 1972, 46 percent were in favor, 37 percent were opposed, and 17 percent did not know. When a 1972 question mentioned "women's liberation groups" and asked women if they were sympathetic to their efforts, 49 percent of Southern women said they were not, 37 percent said they were, and 14 percent were not sure. The problem lies in the title and image, and 9 percent of Southern women who want improved status for women are offended by them. As Mr. Harris says, " . . . the phrase, 'women's liberation' remains an emotionally charged expression with negative implications for many women . . ." who want change but still want to be ladylike about it. The negative reactions included: "women wanting to take over men's roles," "radical, militaristic, revolutionary, aggressive women," "silly and faddish," "women trying to get into things they don't belong in," "bunch of frustrated, insecure, ugly, hysterical, masculine-type women." That list of descriptions would certainly make a woman think twice, but, as we see in the seven point shift in favor of strengthening women's positions, women are looking beyond those labels to the positive and practical aspects of the women's movement.

Forty-six percent favor organizations to strengthen women's participation in politics. Fifty-eight percent describe themselves as not at all active, but 55 percent think women should become more active. Twenty percent think their states will never be ready to elect a woman governor. Thirteen percent think the country will never be ready to accept the appointment of a woman justice to the U.S. Supreme Court and 20 percent never want to see one appointed, though 49 percent are ready for her appointment right now.

There are one hundred thousand elective jobs in the South, including school boards, other municipal offices, state and federal positions. In 1973, black women held one hundred and fifty of them. Nobody knows how many are held by white women.

Sissy Farenthold has just run for governor of Texas again, and she was defeated. Rumor has it that many Alabama women offered for election recently, but I have not heard how they fared. Southern women, Lindy Boggs of Louisiana and Barbara Jordan of Texas, fill two of the region's one hundred and thirty seats in the U.S. Congress.

Almost every Southern state has national women's political caucus groups; the Democratic and Republican parties have made some space for women to advance in the party structures. NOW and the ERA struggle have begun to catch the attention of women who have not paid much attention to politics in the past. Many women's minds were changed favorably toward the equal rights amendment by the arguments and tactics of the anti-ERA women. It is sometimes shocking to hear people speaking in your name, on your behalf, and saying things that do not express your point of view.

Southern women are a little lower in their percentage endorsement of the changing roles of women, but we are pretty close to the rest of the women, and we have had to climb off a rickety pedestal and through a lot of heavy syrup to do it.

A couple of weekends ago, a Mississippi Episcopal church honored its members who were graduating from high school. They lined up in front of the congregation, the dean smiled benignly and asked, "Have you ever seen a prettier bunch of girls or a smarter looking bunch of boys?" Nobody had. And when they graduate from college it is quite likely to be "put the pretty little thing in the stenographer's pool" (she's an honor graduate in political science) and "put that bright boy in the junior executive training program" (he's got B's and C's in political science).

Mr. Harris' study of women and the economy shows "that women's influence . . . is largely confined to *purchasing power*. Few women have the final word when it comes to borrowing, saving and investing. Only in the area of budgeting family expenses do some women make decisions independently of their husbands." "The majority of women report that there's no money left 'for saving, investing and other such things' when 'all the things they have to pay for are taken care of.' " That is how women in all the regions feel, and it would certainly be true of Southern women.

Myths and facts.

And images: Rosa Parks gazing into living rooms from the television screen, sick and tired of being sick and tired. Weeping mothers in Birmingham. Fannie Lou Hamer addressing the Democratic convention in Atlantic City. Myrlie Evers and Coretta King, heads high, veiled in black for their assassinated husbands' funerals. Angela Davis, brilliant and revolutionary, as far away as she can get from Alabama, looking at the world with defiance. Mary Ann Mobley, Miss Mississippi, Miss America. Bobby Gentry and her "Ode to Billie Joe." Billie Jean King trouncing Bobby Riggs. The women of Little Rock forming a howling gauntlet for a lone black student entering Central High. New Orleans women, faces twisted with hatred for three little girls walking into McDonough No. 19 and the solitary first grader dressed for her first day at William T. France Elementary.

The country has seen the worst of us, the rseults of the worst, a touch of make-believe and a touch of talent. There is a substantial body of fine literary work produced by Southern women. There are able women everywhere, women of conscience and ability and achievement. Alice Walker sends her poems and stories up like flowers all over the landscape. Brownie Ledbetter of Arkansas applies her political skills at home in Arkansas and through the NWPC. Winifred Green travels the South working for fair and improved public education. Claire Harvey roams the world as the leader of Churchwomen United seeking peace and understanding for all people.

Are Southern women different? After all the romanticizing and mythmaking are cut away, would anyone say we were really more hospitable, sexier, more devoted to our families, better, worse, happier, unhappier? No.

But, we do have something uniquely in common as Southern women. We have an opportunity furnished by our bitter, bloody past to truly see ourselves, our region, and our relationship to it. We know our worst.

We know that too many of our people are poor. That too many of our babies die. That our prisons and jails are ghastly. That our schools are not good enough. That we make low wages and pay high taxes. That all too often we find ourselves serving our public servants. That parents of many little children have to leave them somewhere while they work. That old people need our help. That racism and sexism, cruelty and isolation exact a price beyond loneliness. That we cannot afford that price.

We know what evil and guilt cost.

And we know what good people can do.

We know because those were Southerners sitting in churches and shabby meeting halls hearing about the rights of American citizens. Southerners marching in Selma. Southerners getting knocked in the head and bombed when they tried to register and vote.

We know because Autherine Lucy was an Alabamian with courage.

We know because Dorothy Tilly and the Association of Southern Women for the Prevention of Lynching set out in 1930 to exert their power to stop the killings. Their power was not economic or political. It was in their minds and hearts, their will and decency.

Today we have a bit more money, a few new skills to add to what the small band of depression era women had. We will have economic power; we will have political power, when we use our minds, our hearts, our wills, and our decency to further our common cause, which is more than feminine, more than Southern.

Statistics quoted in the above essay are from the 1970 United States Census.

Is the Southern Literary
Renascence Over?:
A Sort of Cautionary Epistle

LOUIS D. RUBIN, JR.

LOUIS D. RUBIN, JR.—Louis D. Rubin, Jr., born in 1923, is a native of Charleston, South Carolina, and received his undergraduate education at the College of Charleston and then at the University of Richmond, from which he graduated in 1946, having served three years in the United States Army between his junior and senior years. Rubin then worked for various newspapers, took his M.A. from The Johns Hopkins University in 1949, and worked and taught at Hopkins until 1954, when he received his Ph.D. degree in the Aesthetics of Literature.

From 1954 to 1955 Rubin served as assistant professor of English at The University of Pennsylvania and as executive secretary of the American Studies Association. He then became associate editor of the *Richmond News-leader,* a post he left to assume the chairmanship of the Department of English at Hollins College. Rubin joined the faculty of the University of North Carolina in 1964, where he is presently Distinguished Professor of English.

Rubin has received a number of fellowships, including the Sewanee Fellowship in 1953, the Guggenheim Fellowship in 1957; and the American Council of Learned Societies Fellowship in 1964. He held, for one term, a Fulbright lectureship at the Anglo-American Studies Institute at the University of Aix-Marseille at Nice, France.

A prolific writer, Rubin has contributed numerous essays to both scholarly and popular publications. His books include *Southern Renascence: The Literature of the Modern South* (1953), edited with Robert Jacobs, *Thomas Wolfe: The Weather of His Youth* (1955), *The Faraway Country: Writers of the Modern South* (1963), *The Teller in the Tale* (1967), *The Curious Death of the Novel* (1967), *George W. Cable: The Life and Times of a Southern Heretic* (1969), and most recently *The Writer in the South: Studies in a Literary Community* (1972). He has also written a novel, *The Golden Weather* (1967).

It is not nearly so fashionable as it was, a decade or so ago, to be a specialist in Southern literature. I remember that Allen Tate remarked once that at the University of Minnesota, where he was then a member of the faculty, he was thought of as a kind of exotic. I do not doubt it; but attitudes toward exotics change, and what is exotic one year becomes merely unfashionable a little later. When Allen went to Minneapolis in 1951, to succeed Robert Penn Warren, who in turn was going to Yale, it was considered a highly respectable thing for a large Midwestern university to have a genuine, unreconstructed or only partly reconstructed Southern writer on the staff. I do not believe it is nearly so respectable nowadays. This is not to say that there are not Southern writers on various university faculties, but that it is not *because* they are Southern writers that they are given employment.

Why is this? I can think of numerous reasons, some of which are more important than others. Mainly it comes down, however, to the fact that contemporary Southern literature is not generally thought to be the area of crucial literary activity any more. There are some excellent Southern writers, but the collective authorship of the one-time Solid South no longer exercises the kind of proprietary rights it recently seemed to enforce upon the American literary scene.

Does this mean that there has been a decline in the overall quality of the Southern literary imagination? Is the Southern Literary Renascence that began getting under way just after the First World War now entirely, or almost entirely, concluded?

This is where I come in. I confront the fact that for better or for worse (and I have heard both views receive eloquent expression) I am supposed to be something of an Authority on the literature of the Southern Renascence. If you do something long enough, it does not much matter what, eventually you become locked into the role. Just under twenty-five years ago I took it upon myself to begin writing about the then contemporary Southern literary scene, and today, a quarter-century and fifteen books on Southern topics later, I am still very much at it. From time to time throughout that enterprise, I have found myself placed in the position of being expected to answer the questions cited above. Nor am I alone in this respect; there are several other critics of about my own vintage—Walter Sullivan, C. Hugh Holman, Lewis P. Simpson, to name a few of my betters—who seem to be thought of along roughly the same lines. We have been quoted, cited, praised, disparaged (it is of course always easy to sneer at a critic, unless he is also a successful novelist or poet as well), and at specified times trotted out to speak wisdom upon the survival, or lack of it, of the Southern literary imagination in changing times.

Very well. I propose to suggest that it is time to call a halt to it. While it has lasted it has been a Good Thing for us. But faced once again with the question, Is The Southern Renascence Over?, I for one offer the following answer: I do not know. Furthermore, I do not believe anyone else does, either. And finally, when the question is phrased that way, whether it is or is not over is of no importance at all.

I think I had better explain what I mean.

During the decade following the First World War, as is well known, in the wake of the late H. L. Mencken's famous diagnosis of the intellectual life of the Southern states as being a vast wasteland, there began appearing poems, stories, novels, books by present and recent residents of the region that won national and even international attention. The desert had become a garden. The center of American letters, once located in New England and later in New York, had shifted, as the *Times Literary Supplement* of London noted in retrospect, from Chicago to the South. A notable literature began appearing. It was not that the South was actually beginning to produce writers for the first time in its history; there have always been plenty of Southern writers. Rather, it was that *these* particular Southern writers were good writers, important writers. There is no need for me to call their names here; you know them as well as I. Suffice it to say that we had the best American novelist, Faulkner; the best best-seller, *Gone With The Wind;* the leading literary critics, Ransom, Brooks, Warren, and Tate; the best postwar playwright, Tennessee Williams; several of the better poets; and all these not in isolation, as unique phenomena, but as only the most notable of a whole host of good writers. There were male writers, female writers; white writers, black writers; tragic and comic; lyric, epic, and dramatic; fiction and nonfiction; defenders and prosecutors; eulogists and arraigners; chroniclers of the White-Columned Glory That Was, explicators of the sexual and religious rites of the Poor White Trash; the activists and the escapists; name it, and the South had it.

The question that began presenting itself, by the time of the middle 1930's and with renewed vigor in the 1940's and 1950's when it became possible to look back at how it began, was, *Why?* What caused this cultural phenomenon, the Southern Literary Renascence? Obviously the time and place were somehow involved; there were too many good writers suddenly upon the scene for their advent to have been coincidental, and they shared too many characteristics, attitudes, preoccupations for their art not to have grown, in some important way, out of their environment.

The most plausible explanation, suggested by various earlier commentators, articulated by Allen Tate, and thereafter elaborated upon by numerous others (including myself), was that in the changing over from one kind of society to another, with its attendant deep running consequences in social, political, economic, and religious attitudes and assumptions, the South during the first decades of the twentieth century had posed for its young men and women a special problem in human definition, the answer to which had been given in the language of literature. The older, agricultural South had been settled, ordered, traditionally religious, economically impoverished, sectarian, agrarian, closed. It was preindustrial; it had been deeply rooted in the land, the family had been its dominant social unit, there were established and recognizable lines of caste and class, and there had been a strong sense of historical identification and *pietas*. The impact of the Civil War and the Reconstruction had only confirmed its ways and narrowed its options. While the rest of the nation moved ahead into industrial, urban America, the South had stayed as it was.

Not until the new century was under way had the South begun importantly to change, and it was the impact of the War of 1917-1918 that confirmed its belated reentry into the Union. Towns became cities, cities metropolises; agriculture was displaced by commerce and manufacture; new ideas, new modes, new ways of viewing the world and the social firmament became manifest; the traditional religious, sectarian ordering was severely weakened; new people came in, others went away to see the world beyond the Potomac and the Ohio and came back changed in outlook and attitude. Mass communications, modern transportation drew the rural South into the orbit of the cities and destroyed its self-sufficiency; there was mobility, money, modernism; the old loyalties and pieties were eroded.

That was part of it, but there was more. It involved the South's particular history, with its heritage of slavery, secession, Reconstruction, aristocracy, white supremacy, political separateness. It had engendered fierce loyalty, intense identification. The Southern literary tradition had been long and deeply rhetorical; it had concerned itself with defense and had shied away from introspective examination. But as the traditional South began breaking up and the world beyond its borders opened up once again, the young Southerner for the first time was forced to examine himself, to question his own identity and its relationship to the society around him. In place of rhetoric, the argument with others made from fixed premises, came dialectic, the argument with oneself. The problems of human definition amid social, economic, and political change were fought out within the individual consciousness and took the form of stories about people and places in crisis, poems about the self in the world. In Tate's words, " . . . the South not only reentered the world with the first World War; it looked round and saw for the first time since about 1830 that the Yankees were not to blame for everything." Thus the Southern legend "of defeat and heroic frustration was taken over by a dozen or more first-rate writers and converted into a universal myth of the human condition."

So much for what by now has become a pretty well-known

story. Now clearly this kind of discovery could only have been possible because the Southern writers of the 1920's and 1930's were of both worlds: the new and the old. They were moderns, and the new values and attitudes and ways of viewing their world were informed by the values and attitudes and insights of twentieth-century society, from which they were no longer intellectually and emotionally cut off. At the same time they had the memory, and many of the instincive loyalties and pieties and prejudices and expectations, of the community of their upbringing, a community that was giving way to the modern world only slowly and sometimes painfully as they grew up in it. They were, as Tate and others have said, young men living in the modern world and yet not wholly of it; they saw the past through the eyes of the new and judged it far differently and more critically than their fathers had done, and yet they saw modernity with the perspective of the older Southern community too. Both perspectives were within themselves, not outside; they had a two-way vision, a built-in historical consciousness that permeated their work. I think of Tate's watcher at the cemetery gate, trying to identify his relationship with the dead Confederate soldiers; of the two Quentin Compsons of *Absalom, Absalom!,* the young man preparing to go off to Harvard and the Quentin who was too young to be a ghost but had to be one even so; of Thomas Wolfe's Eugene Gant in Europe, dreaming of the look and sound of a rusty iron railroad bridge back home; of Robert Penn Warren's Jack Burden, trying to fathom the meaning of Cass Mastern's diary; of John Ransom's Captain Carpenter, who would behave chivalrously but keeps finding that the world will not fight fair; and so on. As Faulkner himself put it, "Because it is himself that the Southerner is writing about, not about his environment; who has, figuratively speaking, taken the artist in him in one hand and his milieu in the other and thrust the one into the other like a clawing and spitting cat into a croker sack. And he writes. . . . That cold intellect which can write with calm and complete detachment and gusto of its contemporary scene is not among us. . . ."

If this explanation of what went into the achievement of the

Southern Literary Renascence of the years between the two world wars is valid, then certain corollaries would seem to follow. If it was the image of change, the human response to social and spiritual transformation, that lay at the heart of the artistic vision, then as the South moved further and further in the direction of becoming a modern, urban, secular industrial society and further and further away from the old ordering, its young men and women would be able to draw less often and less intensively upon the division of loyalties and attitudes engendered therefrom. They would necessarily become more and more *of* the new; the older attitudes would be more remote, less a part of their personal vision; and so the conflict that provided the tension between the opposed and contradictory attitudes and assumptions would be severely weakened. If it was the crossing over from the one to the other that made possible the high art, then as the journey drew to its close, as the vessel neared the harbor, the art must by definition cease to partake of the storm and stress of midpassage. The older, rural South had all but become the modern, urban South. No longer was the Southern writer caught between the two contrasting versions of experience. So it would be logical, therefore, to expect that the generations of Southern authors coming along after Faulkner, Wolfe, Warren, Tate, Ransom, Welty, and their contemporaries would be less Southern in their outlook, and more modern, more like the authors of the rest of America.

Thus the question, which has been asked from the middle 1930's onward and which continues to be asked: is the Renascence over? Granted that there will probably continue to be writing in the South, will it be *Southern* writing as we have known it?

To find an answer to this oft-repeated query, what we have done—at any rate what I have done, on various occasions—is to look at the writing of our own generation, those who came into the literary arena after the Second World War, to see how the process was coming along. One scanned the work of such writers as William Styron, Flannery O'Connor, Walker Percy, and others. How did that work differ from the fiction of the previous generation? Did the difference connote a falling-off? Depending on how one responded to the work of these writers, one could come up with widely varying conclusions. Styron was good, the argument went, but his viewpoint was private and existential rather than that of the old dynastic tragic sense; did this then mean that the high drama of the Southern experience was receding and no longer could offer the image for meaningful tragedy? Or did it mean instead that the Southern literary mode was being adapted to a new kind of artistic attitude, thus proving its sustaining powers? No one could question Flannery O'Connor's effectiveness along fairly traditional lines, but did it come because the Southern experience continued to make itself available to newer writers, or because her Roman Catholic allegiance had in effect served to stave off the inevitable erosion of the older mode—producing a kind of lingering remnant, as it were? Since Walker Percy was bent on showing the demise of the old Southern stoic way and since his Christian, existentialist position was predicated upon the perception of the absurdity of the traditional Southern outlook in a changed situation, was this evidence of the death of the South? Or of a creative new way of looking at the continuing South?

One could go at the matter with different assumptions and come up with vastly different conclusions. When I look back, for example, at what my longtime friend Walter Sullivan and I have been writing on the subject these past ten or fifteen years, I get the impression that what Walter has been saying is that *It can't go on any longer,* while the burden of my pontification has been that *It must go on.* I have on various occasions accused Walter of exemplifying the Vanderbilt Apocalyptic School of Southern Literary Interpretation, and if he were a less generous man than he is he might well accuse me of exemplifying the Chapel Hill Pollyanna School of the same. An unkind observer might characterize our differences by saying that he has been insisting that things have been going to Hell in a basket ever since Henry VIII confiscated the monasteries, while I have been insisting desperately that everything is happening for the best in the best of all possible worlds instead of facing up to the evidence visible daily on the front page of my newspaper. I exaggerate, but there is something to this.

But isn't the truth of the matter that Walter Sullivan and I have both, as they say, been Whistling Dixie? Haven't we both—and I mean of course not only the two of us, but the critical positions we have tended to represent—been engaged in our own versions of patriotic literary labor on behalf of what John Ransom referred to in his poem "Antique Harvesters" as "the Proud Lady, with the heart of fire"? What I mean is this. Walter Sullivan, and those of his persuasion, have been setting up or at least identifying something known as Southern virtue and belaboring those who have fallen away from it, which as he says is pretty nearly all of us. I quote from Mr. Sullivan: "Within the larger ambiance of our spiritual deprivation, the South has retained something of its separate identity and in weakened form some of the conditions that helped to produce the literary renascence. Good manners remain and the love of the land and an innate sense of mystery. But the old strength, the vitality that was inherent in the homogeneous culture is gone, and I see no immediate hope for its restoration." Meanwhile, Louis Rubin, and those who share his approach, have by contrast been insisting that, no indeed, it is not dead, and anyone who dares say it is is a blind worshiper of the past. I quote from Mr. Rubin, in an address given at The University of Alabama campus over ten years ago in a symposium on "The Deep South in Transformation":

> Surely the process of adjusting to new experience, of learning how to square old ideals, attitudes, and values with their embodiment in new and different circumstances and institutions is still far from being over. It would hardly be accurate to declare that the South has by now mastered and assimilated its urban experience, and that the travail of transition is no longer taking place within our minds and hearts. Everything we know and read and see would indicate otherwise. So if literary achievement thrives on the problems of definition involved in the turmoil of social change, there is still plenty of it left for the younger writers. ("The Literature of a Changing South," *The Deep South in Transformation,* p. 159)

With all respects to the feeling of the author, I think that is pretty bad prose. But what it says, it seems to me, is that what we like about the South in the past will continue to exist, and so Southern literature as we have known it is safe for another generation or two at least. And that, I am afraid, is also worship of the past, though in slightly disguised form.

Sullivan's position has at least the merit of being logical, while my own cannot be said even to be that. But both are, I think, as critical positions predicated on quite shaky premises. Let me dissect my own position first, and then I will get to work on Sullivan's. It seems perfectly obvious to me, when I look at it with some perspective and more rue, that what I have been attempting to insist is that change is the hallmark of contemporary Southern literature, but that even though the change has been going on at a tremendous rate the literature can be expected to remain essentially the same. This is known as attempting to have it both ways. If the name of the game is change, from one kind of South into another, then how could one possibly expect the literature that succeeded the 1920's, 1930's, and 1940's not to be importantly different from what came before? It is true that on occasions I have in effect conceded this, but even so my rhetoric has been all in the direction of seeking to tie in what Styron, O'Connor, Percy, et al., have done with what their predecessors achieved before then. There *are* ties, and important ones; but surely, if the thesis is valid, it would be much more to the point to examine the ways in which the change has been registered, in order to understand both what was going on and what it means about the nature of Southern experience in our time. That would seem to be what is important.

In the instance of Mr. Sullivan, we have something of the same kind of misplaced zeal, only in reverse. His approach has been to assume the literary importance of the generation of Faulkner, Warren, Welty, Wolfe, et al., and then because the later writers have failed to produce the kind of literature—not simply good literature, but the same kind of good literature—as their predecessors, he has repeatedly proclaimed the decline and fall

of the Southern imagination. Well, that might well be so, but what
does it prove? Might he not have invested his critical energies
much more profitably in concentrating upon what is being written,
on its own terms, rather than what used to be written but isn't
any more? Surely the work of his and my contemporaries, whatever its merit, deserves to be read in its own right, as constituting
all that we have of Southern literature in our own time, rather than
being summarily dismissed as unworthy of the South of Faulkner
and his contemporaries.

In both Mr. Sullivan's and my instance—and I use the two of
us as emblematic of a tribe of commentators—there is a very
simple explanation of what we have been doing. It is what I
suggested a bit earlier. We have been behaving like the literary
patriots we are. We have been defending Southern virtue. I have
been reading the contemporaries as if they were essentially of the
same generaton as their predecessors because I wished to yield no
ground to the enemy. I have not wanted to admit, either to myself
or to such public as I have, that the Renascence might be over
and done, that it flowered in a time of soul-searing Southern
transition, and that it both delineated and ornamented that transition. I did not *want* for it to be over. I had a stake, emotional and
perhaps even professional, in its not ending—and this even though
I have thoroughly approved of some of the most important and
far-reaching changes that have taken place in Southern society.
My ultimate response was based on patriotic zeal, not literary or
social analysis. This is why I say that the quesiton, Is The Southern
Literary Renascence Still Continuing, is unimportant and meaningless when phrased in that way. What is being asked at such
times is whether the Bonnie Blue Flag will continue to wave
triumphantly in the literary big wind and the wise boys who
constitute the publishing industry in New York will thus have to
continue, against all their inclinations, to face the fact that though
the important books are merchandized out of the big city, they
are written in the Southern provinces. Being an optimist (or
perhaps a wishful thinker), I have wanted to go on in the high
style, because I liked it that way. Being a pessimist (or perhaps a

realist); Mr. Sullivan has been quick to insist that it has not, could not, and is therefore an emblem of how we have come upon crass times through failure to retain the old ways. Well, the times may indeed be crass, and the writers may win no Nobel Prizes, but Mr. Sullivan might well ask himself whether, if it is contemporary literature that we would deal with, we have any viable alternative other than the literature actually being written around us. As Allen Tate once suggested in a poem, whatever the difficulties of the present, there is not much profit in making a profession out of setting up the ravenous grave in the house we must live in. And at the same time, there is not much sense in trying to claim that Styron is the Faulkner of his generation, when he manifestly is not, could not be, and, if he is to be of much literary importance to anyone, should not be.

What I am saying is that we have got to look at Southern literature as an ongoing thing, closely related to developing Southern experience and taking its concerns and lineaments out of that experience, and not as a static patriotic act or as a regional showpiece. What the writers of the South are presently writing *is* Southern literature. The fact that this literature bears resemblance to the writings of Faulkner, Wolfe, Ransom, and their contemporaries is not primarily what makes it important or noteworthy; to make any real sense out of understanding that literature and using it to interpret the Southern experience, one must take precisely the opposite approach. One must make such use of the earlier writers as can help to illuminate the contemporaries, and not vice versa. From the point of view of contemporary Southern literature and in terms of that objective, Styron is not interesting because he follows the lead of Faulkner, if that is indeed what he does; Faulkner is interesting because he prefigures Styron. One must not view the body of the present-day Southern literature as the latest development of the great tradition; one must view the tradition as helping to make possible the present-day literature, and when that is not what has happened, the job is to concentrate on the contemporary writers and not the tradition.

I am not proposing any kind of ahistorical or antihistorical

approach; I am by no means insisting that the past is a bucket of
ashes, as Carl Sandburg once so felicitously put it. What I am
saying is that in terms of seeking to understand the present, one
should approach the past as contributing to the present, but not
view the present as either confirming or denying the worth of the
past. Anything else is an exercise in futility. We need a new
generation of critics of Southern literature who will look at what
is being written in the South today in its own right and not
against a scale of measurement made up of the novels of William
Faulkner and the poems of the Nashville Fugitives and their contemporaries. Only in that way can one understand and judge what
is now being written.

I say, *one* should do this, not that *I* could do it. The fact is that
I cannot. It is not what I know. For the truth is, of course, that
the true contemporary Southern literature is not even that being
produced by Styron, Walker Percy, Madison Jones, James Dickey,
and the like, not to speak of Eudora Welty and Robert Penn
Warren. These writers are all in their late forties or fifties. They
are doing impressive work, and I have no doubt that none of them
is close to being used up yet as an author. It is possible, too, that
I might still have something useful to say about them from time
to time. But what the student who would understand the present
South through its literature really needs to do is to begin paying a
great deal more attention than is now being paid to the Southern
writers who are presently in their twenties and thirties. *They* are
the writers of the contemporary South. I will name a few names:
Sylvia Wilkinson, Ernest Gaines, A. R. Ammons, James Seay,
William Harmon, Bertha Harris, Lee Smith, Cormac McCarthy,
Fred Chappell, Jane Logan, Henry Taylor, R. H. W. Dillard, Van
K. Brock, Margaret Gibson, Miller Williams, John William
Corrington.

Have I missed some important writers? Have I named some
not really worth bothering with? If so, there is a very good reason.
I do not really know them. By this I do not mean that there are
not some of the group whose work I admire very much, but the
truth is that when that is so, the familiarity is primarily the result

of extraliterary factors, usually personal friendship. As a generation of authors, they do not interest me. That is a hard thing to
say, but it is so. They do not interest me, not through any fault
of their own whatever, but because I am simply too set in my
interests to be interested in them. What I know, and might have
something useful to say about, is not them, but their predecessors,
my own generation and their forebears of the Southern Renascence.
For me to continue to pose as an informed student of contemporary
Southern literature is to fly under false colors. I am not that any
more, and cannot be, and if there is anything that I can say for
myself by way of extenuation, it is that at least I begin to realize
it.

I believe, in short, that when the evaluation of contemporary
literature is involved, there comes a time when only a contemporary can do it, and that in the case of contemporary Southern literature, when we have so massive and formidable a tradition of excellence in the immediate past, the problem is rendered
doubly difficult. The prudent and proper response of the commentator who finds himself in my position, therefore, is to be
very, very wary of passing judgments. The appropriate course of
action, I believe, is to follow the precedent set by Edmund Wilson.
You will recall that during the 1920's and 1930's, Wilson was
the leading interpreter of the literature of his generation, the
avant-garde of the period, to the informed public. In books such
as *Axel's Castle, The Wound and the Bow,* and in the magnificent
review essays he wrote for the *New Republic* and other magazines,
Wilson did more, perhaps, than anyone else to make such writers
as Joyce, Eliot, Fitzgerald, Hemingway, Yeats, Proust, Stein, and
Valéry available to American readers. He was their champion,
and he was able to show the reading public how to read their
work. If he was often wrong in the details, he was unerringly right
in the assessment of value he placed on their work. But beginning
in the late 1930's and the 1940's, Edmund Wilson largely turned
away from the contemporary literary scene. He would not do
for the authors of the 1940's and 1950's what he had done for
the previous generation—be their explicator and interpreter.

Instead he moved backward, into the past, and began to explore how the writers of his generation got where they were, through understanding *their* predecessors and showing how his own generation fitted into the tradition. He produced long memoirs and reassessments of such writers as Edna St. Vincent Millay, James Branch Cabell, George W. Cable, and others. He wrote books such as *Patriotic Gore.*

I have heard people describe Wilson's turning away from his role of interpreter of the contemporary as a kind of betrayal of office; they saw his refusal to do for the next generation of authors what he had done for his own as a real deprivation. But I must say that the older I get, the better I understand why Wilson did what he did and the wiser his decision seems to me. For Wilson did not *know* the new writers of the 1940's and 1950's in the way that he knew those of the 1920's and 1930's; their imaginative experience was not his. In crucial respects they had not shared in his circumstance, and he could not share theirs. What he knew was Hemingway and Eliot and Fitzgerald and the time and place that produced them and himself. And so what he did was to use that knowledge to search backward in time, to examine the world out of which they and he had come, to see and understand more clearly the ties between his day and the earlier writers. That was what he now had to contribute and what he set out to provide. In the years of his young manhood, when the writers of his generation were in the process of producing their major work, he could see and explain to the reading public *why* they had to do things differently and what it was that they were trying to do. As he grew older, what he began to discover more and more clearly was the relationship of his generation's writers to the writers of an earlier time; it was no longer a matter of why they were and had to be different; what he could also see and show now was the continuity. But if instead of going back, he had tried to continue to interpret the new writing as it appeared, what he would have been doing was seeing the writers of the next generation primarily in terms of his own; and since he understood the achievement of his own contemporaries so much better the younger writers would have suffered by comparison. He was wise enough, I think, to realize that he was not imaginatively involved in the excitement of new discovery in poetry and fiction any longer and was therefore not really interested in what the younger writers had to say. So he made the decision to stick with what he knew and to find out more about that. From being an interpretive critic of contemporary literature, he changed into a critical and cultural historian.

And something like that, I propose, is what we had better do. We had better be honest enough to recognize that the new writing of the 1960's and 1970's does not and can not hold the interest and offer the excitement of discovery to us that the writing of our own generation was able to do. We must not allow ourselves to play William Dean Howells to the current generation's Theodore Dreiser, or Edmund Gosse to their James Joyce. When we hear ourselves remarking, upon reading the new work of a young writer who has gotten very good reviews, that we can not see anything to him, that he seems vulgar or trashy or formless to us, we ought to remember how our own elders were saying precisely the same thing about Faulkner or Wolfe or Warren or Styron or Percy and how blind they then seemed to us and how outraged we were. Ah, we might reply, but so-and-so *is not* Faulkner and such-and-such *is not* a Styron. True, and since what we know is Faulkner and Styron, we will inevitably try to make so-and-so and such-and-such into Faulkner and Styron and then complain because they are not. I am not of course maintaining that it is inevitable or even likely that the newer generation is going to produce writers comparable to Faulkner and Wolfe and the others in stature and importance, but I am saying that *if* that did happen we would probably be the last to recognize it when we saw it.

I call, therefore, for a moratorium, not on the continued criticism of the contemporary Southern literary scene, but on its continued criticism in terms of Is the Southern Renascence Over? Maybe it is, maybe it is not; but merely to ask the question in those terms is to place a crippling liability upon the ability to interpret and understand the newer generation of Southern writers. And I

suggest, to myself and to other commentators whose chief interest
has been in the writers of the continuing Renascence, that it may
well be that we have provided just about all we have to contribute
to the fount of information on the subject and would do much
better to direct our explorations backward rather than forward in
time. What we need to understand is what the writers of the 1920's
and 1930's and their successors of the 1940's and 1950's came
out of, not where their successors are going. What we can do, if
we are imaginative enough and wise enough, is to draw the connections much more closely than they have been drawn between
the writing of our time and that which preceded it. We can try to
understand and explain just what was involved in the momentous
move from rhetoric to dialectic, to use Allen Tate's formulation,
whereby the Southern literary imagination took on the universal
image and coloration of important literature that hitherto had
mostly eluded it. In order to do that we must increase our understanding of the literature and the life of the older South—not so
much the ante-bellum South as that of the late nineteenth and early
twentieth centuries. It was against the values of that milieu that
the writers of the Southern Renascence were rebelling; as *The
Fugitive* put it in a manifesto in its first issue,

> THE FUGITIVE flees from nothing faster than from the high-
> caste Brahmins of the Old South. Without raising the question
> of whether the blood in the veins of its editors runs red, they
> at any rate are not advertising it as blue; indeed, as to pedigree,
> they cheerfully invite the most unfavorable inference from the
> circumstances of their anonymity. (*The Fugitive,* 1, 1)

To those high-caste Brahmins who populated the Southern literary
scene in the 1920's what those young Southerners were doing with
their puzzlingly modern poems and their highly shocking novels
must indeed have seemed illegitimate. But from the perspective of
a later generation, we can see that not only was the lineage pretty
much impeccable, but never before had the literary vine borne
such distinguished fruit. Let us, therefore, concentrate on showing
how and why that happened and leave the verdict on the contemporary scene to those who can understand it.

If we do not, we are likely to find ourselves saying some pretty foolish things. I think, for example, of Ellen Glasgow, who during the early decades of our century waged so brave and vigorous a literary campaign against the genteel school of Southern writing and of whom Stuart Sherman wrote in 1925 that "realism crossed the Potomac 25 years ago, going north." It was Miss Glasgow's dictum that what the South needed most was blood and irony, and she did her best to give it both qualities. Yet the times changed, and late in her life we discover Miss Glasgow deposing as follows:

> . . . Heaven forbid that I should set out as a champion of that forlorn hope, human behaviour. One may admit that the Southern States have more than an equal share of degeneracy and deterioration; but the multitude of half-wits, and whole idiots, and nymphomaniacs, and paranoiacs, and rakehells in general, that populate the modern literary South could flourish nowhere but in the weird pages of melodrama.

She had in mind, of course William Faulkner and Erskine Caldwell (she was unable to tell the difference between them). Because she could not understand what those writers and their contemporaries were up to, she wound up using just about the same kind of argument against the writers of the 1920's and 1930's that had once been used against her, and for much the same reasons. It seems to me that when we older commentators begin inveighing against the deterioration of the literary imagination in our time, we are in considerable danger of sounding just as absurd. The point is that we do not *know* these new writers, because we cannot sufficiently engage ourselves in their experience, and it is better for them and for us to leave the matter alone. Let us not become for the new generation the Old Fogies that the writers of our generation had to combat.

For if there is one thing that is certain, it is that this literature business must go on. It cannot be frozen permanently in any mode or attitude, no matter how attractive. Its essence is the response of men and women to the demands and confusions of an always changing human situation, and we can no more expect it to remain suspended forever in the style of Faulkner and his contemporaries than it could have been in the style of Thomas Nelson Page and Ellen Glasgow. It is quite true that there are good times and bad times and that in the ultimate judgment of literary history there are many instances in which the writing of one time proved to be more distinguished than that of another. It is very easy, therefore, and very tempting, to see our own time, and that of our immediate forebears, as the good time and what follows as increasingly less good to the extent that it deviates from the standard. Now it may well be that—but how are we, of all persons, likely to be able to make that judgment with any accuracy, grounded so thoroughly as we are in the imaginative responses of our own generation?

I would conclude this cautionary epistle, therefore, with a quotation. The author is enumerating the shortcomings of contemporary youth:

> The first is a growing tendency of the age to avoid every species of physical exertion which can be escaped by any means short of deception. There is a popular term for this disposition, which is hardly flattering to ears polite, but very appropriate, viz.: laziness.
>
> The author of this article has enjoyed an opportunity of witnessing the vast extent to which the young men of the State have fallen under its influence, and the natural consequence is, that they are incapable of standing ordinary fatigue—that is, the ordinary fatigue of a soldier. . . . Eternal vigilance is the price of liberty, and those who cannot make this slight sacrifice are unworthy of the blessing. The security of the commonwealth is not to be endangered, that a few idlers may squirt tobacco-juice over the pavement.

We all know that the advent of the automobile and the two-car family has produced a generation of youths who have forgotten how to walk and who expect to be chauffeured everywhere by indulgent parents. We know, too, that the old respect for authority that we knew in our young manhood has eroded badly. But that indictment was not composed last week and excerpted from this morning's paper. It appeared in *Russell's Magazine* in the city of

Charleston, South Carolina, in March of the year 1860. I suspect that the author was William Gilmore Simms, though it is unsigned. At the time Simms was in his middle fifties. But whether it was Simms or another of his contemporaries who wrote it, I hope it is obvious that the verdict given by posterity as to the worth of those deplorably lazy young Southerners of 1860 turned out to be rather more favorable than one would have anticipated from reading the contemporary assessment in *Russell's Magazine.* I suggest, therefore, that in general it is a good thing for middle-aged critics to leave the contemporary scene to those who understand it and, both as social and literary commentators, go easy with the *Ubi Sunt* motif.

Coming to Terms with
Another New South

DAVID MATHEWS

DAVID MATHEWS—David Mathews is a native of Grove Hill, Alabama. He received his A.B. in History and Classical Greek and M.A. in Education from The University of Alabama. After serving as an officer in the United States Army, Mathews completed his Ph.D. in the History of American Education at Columbia University in 1965 and returned to The University of Alabama. Mathews held a number of administrative posts in addition to his responsibilities as lecturer in the Department of History. He was appointed executive assistant to the president in 1966, executive vice president in 1968, and he was made president of the University in 1969. He is currenlty on leave, serving as Secretary of Health, Education, and Welfare.

Mathews has continued to teach and write in the area of American History and has provided vigorous leadership to The University of Alabama. His interests are not parochial, however, and are not simply limited to the administration of the University. He is especially active in exploring the roles that institutions of higher education can play in relationship to public policy developments on a state and regional basis.

In his efforts to relate universities to public policy formation, he has served as chairman of the Birmingham Branch of the Federal Reserve System, and his interest in the widest possible application of education is reflected in his membership on the National Programming Council for Public Television, because of the opportunities for adult education through television, and in his national educational activities as a trustee of the Kettering Foundation. Mathews also serves on advisory bodies of the American Council on Education and the National Association of State Universities and Land-Grant Colleges. Most recently Mathews has served on the Commission on the Future of the South, Southern Growth Policies Board, and it is from this vantage point that he views and comments upon the latest "New South."

Southerners of every generation have the inevitable task of coming to terms with the always changing definition of the "South." This process of definition is at any time in the history of the

South a powerful intellectual and cultural and political force. Once set, any definition, even if not accurate, is a powerful schoolmaster for the next generation of Southerners.

My approach to commenting on the Rising South is much more personal than those of the other speakers; it is essentially to give an account of my own intellectual journey in reaction to the New South that began to emerge in the early 1970's.

I began my journey, naturally enough, by first analyzing other New Souths. In previous essaying that I have done, I have questioned early technological definitions of progress for the New South of the Grady era, and I have taken issue with the more recent tendency to model the South's progress on national standards. My efforts have centered finally in trying to blend old traditions into new and useful realities by the deliberate use of the myth-building capacity of the South, which has so often been put to reactionary ends. This effort has, in turn, resulted in a sorting of Southern traditions into those that need preserving and those that do not.

My final comments in this essay are those I have also made to the Commission on the Future of the South, which, in the summer of 1974 was preparing a blueprint of growth policies for thirteen Southern states. The commission, on which I sat as Alabama's representative, was an agency of the Southern Growth Policies Board. The path from that commission led to issues far more mundane and immediate than the rather philosophic questions I had examined before, but the theme stayed much the same. If there is to be a new, and better, South for the 1970's and beyond, then that future, even to be as utopian as we want it, may still need to resemble the best things we can now see out of our own windows.

For the interpretative comments that tie together five years of articles and speeches dealing with the concept of the New South, I am indebted to Ms. Sheryl Overlan, who was working with me as an editorial assistant in 1973. The research, and most importantly the arguing, that goes into sorting through all the ideas about New Souths was made possible by the assistance of Dr. Robert H. McKenzie and Dr. Joan North.

EARLIER NEW SOUTHS

During the late sixties, the South was again showing signs of "rising." As if in celebration of this newest potential for economic gain and a better life, a "New South" again was heralded by Southern politicians, businessmen, and academicians. Unlike the industrial dominated "New South" proclaimed by Henry Grady during the 1880's, the current "New South" was founded on more than the presence and promise of new industry. Social developments in other sections of the country enhanced the image of the South. The South no longer was viewed as the center for race problems. Race riots and demonstrations dotted Northern cities for several hot and long summers and received media coverage, not only in the northern United States, but also abroad. Race was no longer only "the Southern problem." Just as significant, there was a gradual realization in America during this time that "progress" was a two-edged sword and that there was something desirable about the "old" ways.

The promise of another New South and a new national attitude toward the South needs to be viewed through the perspective of earlier New Souths. Those earlier ventures represented a common attempt by Southerners to improve their living conditions, even though they failed to acknowledge important human factors in the Southern milieu.

The South has more than once in its history been identified with a quest for renewal. In the 1500's, Ponce DeLeon sought the fountain of youth in Florida; in the days of the early Republic, Jefferson sought pure democracy in the yeoman farmer; in the 1850's, William Lowndes Yancey and other young romantics sought aristocratic idealism in a plantation-dominated independent nation; in the 1880's and 1890's Henry Grady and his colleagues sought economic plenty in textile and iron mills; and in the 1920's and 1930's, Allen Tate and the Agrarians sought refuge from idustrialized materialism in the South's heritage and tradition .

This original "New South," a phenomenon that occurred between the 1880's and the 1930's, also boasted of kicking regional habits, of planting industry at every crossroad, and of being "on the move." With four hundred new cotton mills smoking on the Southern countryside, hundreds of poor families receiving wages, the pressure taken off the flooded agricultural market, things did look good.

But somehow in that New South, we became so caught up in our own propaganda that we forgot to look at what we really had. And what we really had was just an extension of the poverty of the plantation system shifted into an industrialized framework. A "family wage" in the new industrialized South meant that every member of the family who wanted to eat, even the women and children, had to work long and hard for the money to pay the commissary for food. And while the image of the South prospered, the people who made that image possible, the cheap labor force, were a straggly, tubercular lot, and not a credit to anyone.

We should have learned from earlier New Souths that progress without people was just so much technology. And if all of the South's pasts are distilled, they yield, for me, that one strong lesson.

What then, or even where, is the South? Is the South Jefferson's yeoman farmer in the foothills of the Piedmont? Is the South Yancey's independent nation, a nation in essence of Black Belt and Delta planters? Is the South Grady's bustling mills in cities like Atlanta and Birmingham? Is the South Tate's heritage in the hearts of those who love it?

Perhaps Allen Tate, a poet, gives us the best clue as to where to seek the best South. The Tates have been those who have understood that we need to examine carefully the history, the legends, the tradition of the South, and to choose from among them those qualities that can impart individuality and, above all, humanity to the modern world, a world that so often seems to

thunder over us in a mass of computer cards, plastic, and un-
collected garbage.

The Search for a New Blueprint

By 1970, it was clear that the South had to get on with its future
and that neither the ante-bellum past nor the era of the old New
South was a completely adequate guide. Indeed, for Southerners
in the 1970's the search for a new blueprint is of paramount importance.

Drawing that blueprint, however, is very difficult because, for
one thing, it requires that the South harmonize a multitude of
apparently dissonant factors. In a 1969 speech to the Hunstville
Community Council, I used the city of Huntsville to illustrate
those opposing factors; Huntsville, Alabama, is a microcosm for
the transitional problems occurring throughout the South—in
fact, throughout the country. The past and the future, the old
South and the new, localism and nationalism, an agrarian and an
urban way of life, public and private enterprise, the hum of
technology and the heartbeat of people all cross in Huntsville.
Historically, Huntsville was one of the oldest centers of ante-
bellum Alabama, and its heritage is still very much evident in its
architecture. Yet, there is no more striking contrast to an ante-
bellum mansion than a Saturn V rocket. Huntsville, old as it is, is
involved in the newest, most imaginative venture of human technology. This community, like so many in the South, has both
a bond to the past and a commitment to the future.

People everywhere are trying to live in a world characterized
by dramatic, cruel, explosive, frustrating, exciting, promising contrasts between what has been and what may be. We all turn to
the past for stability, but we are all forced out of it by the present.
For Southerners, this is an especially wrenching dilemma.

Such stresses and contrasts are common to the times and are
present in both the Northern and Southern cultures. But there was,
and still is, a tendency for Southerners to follow the approaches
already in use in other sections of the country in dealing with
common problems. That propensity, ironically, exists side by side

with rabid disavowals of the ways of "outsiders." Such imitativeness robs the South of both creativity and effectiveness and needs to be challenged.

It is very common in the South to model ourselves after what the nation has acclaimed to be the most prosperous, the most fashionable, and, presumably, the best. I remember still the faded sign above the clothes in a small department store in the southern part of this state. "Latest New York Fashions," it assured us. It is not uncommon to hear Southern college presidents say that their aim is to be the Harvard of the South. It is not uncommon to hear civic boosters speak of larger, more bustling municipalities. The South has certainly suffered terribly from being too parochial, too closed, but the only alternative we seem to have is to be exactly like everybody else.

The South still has some clean air, pure water, and telephones that work. Above all, we have people who smile, who have hope, who are courteous, who are hard-working, people who have known despair, perhaps hunger, but who are accustomed to meeting problems head on and believe that problems can be solved.

Our concern is how to solve our problems—rural development, for example—while avoiding the urban problems presently confronting the Northeast and the West Coast. Beyond the benefits of electricity, indoor plumbing, and the consolidated school, there lies some point of diminishing social return. How to approach that point without passing it—that is, how to achieve a harmonious balance between the benefits of urban and rural life—is the problem now facing the South. We want industry and growth and increased wealth, but we want these things while still retaining all the virtues of our life-style, in which we have long taken pride.[1]

THE SOUTH AND THE NATIONAL EXPERIENCE

In order for the Southerner to influence his destiny, it is necessary for him to see his past in better perspective, and, in searching for blueprints among those available from the national experience, such a perspective on the South and the nation is essential. In particular, I think it is important that the South is really an anomaly in the American experience and that its history is more akin to older nations, which have run the gamut from youthful success to mature resignation.

For most of its history, the South has been viewed in stereotyped images. The motion picture *Gone with the Wind* has enjoyed such immense international popularity that millions have assumed that the romantic and tragic land of the movie is the real South. There is a texture of contradictions and subtleties to the Southland, so much so that the region affords observers with not merely one oversimplified image but with a host of stereotypes, often contradictory to one another.

To understand more clearly why the South is considered unique within the American experience, some thought should be given to the American experience itself and its unusual relationship to the world.

"Nothing in all history had ever succeeded like America, and every American knew it," observed Henry Steele Commager, a distinguished American historian, in speaking of the United States of the late nineteenth century. Indeed, America has been imbued with a sense of destiny for success that permeates its national character, and until very recently the fates seemed to cooperate with that conviction.

The American "success story" was repeatedly reaffirmed in individual citizens' rise to achievement, in victorious wars, and by material wealth, leading one of our best historians, Arthur Schlesinger, Jr., to conclude twenty years ago that the American character "is bottomed upon the profound conviction that nothing in the world is beyond its power to accomplish." One of the more obvious proofs of the nation's success is the country's history of economic abundance, which led another American historian to dub Americans "people of plenty."

The United States as a whole has for most of its history also conceived of itself as the epitome of innocence. From its beginning, the United States has seen itself as another chance for the world. The blessings of nature and an unbroken series of national successes in settlement, trade, and warfare reinforced the concept of innocence. How could evil suceed so well?

It is this preoccupation with smiling success that has obstructed the nation's comprehension of the South, a section that has not shared in the country's historical good fortune. The South's defeat in the Civil War and its subsequent experiences of frustration and failure in the economic, political, and social realms separate the South from the nation's successes.

Above all, perhaps, the South has lived with guilt. The South fought a war tied to the anachronistic institution of human slavery and a way of life that was linked to that institution. The South has wrestled with the problem of racial prejudice for most of its existence, and its attempts to resolve racial problems have, with very few exceptions, been judged as out-of-step with the rest of the nation.[2]

In recent years, however, the wheels of America's blind, optimistic progress have begun to show signs of wear. The corollary of the progress syndrome—that those who have not kept up are surely somehow backward, even inferior—has also been up for reexamination.

In our time, the American dream of perfection and unlimited possibility has been warped. We have experienced vigorous questioning of our most basic assumptions about what constitutes progress and the good life. And we have suffered these ills, as Job did, even though believing ourselves, like Job, "just and blameless."

Coupled with the recent weakening of its psychological position, the United States has encountered real physical and economic difficulties. The nation's foreign trade position is revealing faults, and perhaps most important of all the realization is dawning that the nation's ecological frontiers are closing. Along with the rest of the civilized world, the United States is learning that the globe's resources have limits. These sobering factors have been decisive in whittling away the American frontier psychology.

Concurrent with this process of disillusionment, the nation has expressed renewed interest in the South. Much of this interest is predicated on the fact that the South now offers the nation another business frontier. Industry has been moving South increasingly since World War II, and the region provides the nation with an area that still has relatively unpolluted water systems and reasonably clean air.

Even more significant, however, the South's experience offers the nation the possibility of better understanding its own evolving predicament. C. Vann Woodward, perhaps the leading historian of the South, pointed out in the early 1950's that the history of the South has much to teach the nation, for the experience of the South more closely parallels that of the rest of the world than does the unique history of success and plenty that have characterized the nation as whole. Having coped with success followed by disillusionment, defeat, scorn, and rebuilding, the South has undergone a range of collective human experience more comparable to that of the older nations of the world than to America itself.[3]

This more positive view of the South's uniqueness is not only useful but immensely satisfying. In fact, in the 1970's young progressives, rather than older reactionaries, are talking confidently of the South's leadership in political, economic, and even racial progress for the country.

But the region's new found optimism is troublesome because it borders on a cockiness that the seriousness of the problem of the seventies will not allow. There is always the danger of glossing over those ancient regional propensities that have left the South characterized by racial turmoil, poverty, defensive parochialism, and the nation's meagerest educational opportunities.

Rather than simply pushing the South's old traditions into the background or uncritically embracing the "American Way," the 1970's are a proper time for a new statement of Southern traditions in relation to current issues.

THE VARIETY OF SOUTHERN TRADITIONS

Southern traditions may be divided into two categories: either they have the potential for contributing to a new and better South, and so a new vision, or they are detrimental, dragging down the Southerner's efforts to improve his condition. Understanding these traditions for their worth or lack of worth is one basis for forming a rational course of action in creating a "New South."

Our efforts to describe a "New South" can never be complete. This time we must choose causes that are just and have a future. We must choose them deliberately and realistically. We must, if need be, create our future not by abandoning our past but by realizing that all of our traditions are two-sided coins and that the very tendencies that have made Southerners reactionary could, indeed, have at times made them progressive. We must use myths, but we must not do what we have done time and time again— turn from reality to romanticism. The people of the South are keenly aware that they must once again influence their own destiny.[4]

The "times" in the 1970's reflect some loss of purpose, some erosion of confidence, some collapse of community. To restate the Southern traditions, to speak to those dilemmas, is a very legitimate use of the New South phenomenon. And there are certainly qualities in the South's heritage that can be good models:

Leading a cause—The South has been a land of causes throughout its history. Not all of our causes have been well-chosen, but we have repeatedly dedicated ourselves to purposes above and beyond our immediate existence in the hope of influencing our future. In contrast, the United States today is somewhat unsure of its mission and of its ability to influence its own destiny. The South should have much to say about choosing wise and unwise causes, and it is in the South that a desire to influence our own destiny and the future is obviously prevalent.

Pride and independence—these are both hallmarks of the South that could well be revived for use as antidotes to a disabling sense of dependence and despair. Certinly Southerners can trade more confidently on their spirit of independence. And certainly the quality that has made us defiant can be put to far more constructive ends. We must also preserve our sense of pride, a sense of working hard and of doing a job well, whether it results in a straight furrow or a good sermon. Pride keeps people involved until the job at hand is done and done well. Pride makes people "pitch in" rather than "drop out."

Hospitality—There are some very modern lessons to be learned even from the very oldest Southern traditions, even from things as corny as Southern hospitality. Politeness—and I am not speaking of meaningless form—is social insurance against the destructiveness that inevitably comes from the abrasion and friction of human competition.

Loving the land— Publicists of the South have long emphasized the attractiveness of our land and climate. We should take this boast to heart. We used to blame most of our economic troubles on the destruction wrought by Yankees during the Civil War. But the Yankees did not destroy our air, our water, or our land. Yet, we in our own mad dash for industrialization stand in danger of destroying the very irreplaceable treasures the Civil War never touched.

Community and home—Southerners have a unique sense of time and place, of belonging, of community. Southerners have roots. They have an identity. A Southerner—whatever his station, whatever his color—has a "home."[5]

THE HUMAN YARDSTICK

Of all the lessons of the Southern experience, what we learn about the efficacy of human hopefulness is the most instructive because the rarest quality in America this year is hope: the ability to believe in, to be confident that the future will be better than the present. Not only is hope a rare quality, but for an individual to be identified with it is as out of fashion as wearing spiked heels or narrow ties. Dreaming dreams is definitely "out." The young today are tempted by cruel cynicism and are drawn toward a vacuum of apathy. Those older talk less of the future, more of the present; less of the ideal, more of the immediate gain; less of their dreams, more of their fears. And those who defend the good that is, or ask for some historical perspective to view our plight, or dare talk about doing the impossible are viewed with utter distrust.

If the ability, the courage, the capacity to look confidently to the future—to hope—exists anywhere in the country today, it may exist most in our section, the South. Amazingly, surprisingly, reported the *New York Times* in a recent aritcle by Pat Watters entitled "Way Up South in the Land of Hope," Southerners have retained the art of hoping uncorrupted by the current national penchant for cynicism.

The hopefulness of the South is not unrealistic or shallow, and there is a history here that can be used to great and good purpose. Not to dare and not to dream would leave us and the nation without what we so desperately need—a new vision of the possible and the necessary and a new spirit of hopefulness.[6]

Our "New South" comes when the nation is far from peaceful; in fact, perhaps for the first time in recent history the nation is experiencing the social unrest and the economic frustration thought to be peculiar to our section. It comes when the South is actually enjoying greater economic growth than many sections and far less distress from such plights as chronic unemployment.

Collateral for the future is not so much in our natural resources (we have changed our position on that issue) but in ourselves— our sense of place and community, our tradition of civility and warmth, and our legacy of caring and commitment.

From Ideals to Problems

As I mentioned earlier, my most recent encounter with the New South has been through serving as Alabama's representative on the Commission of the Future of the South, an agency of the Southern Growth Policies Board, which in turn was a creation of thirteen Southern state governments. The topics discussed by the commission were not style and culture, but land use and transportation development and planning strategies and human resource conservation. These conversations led to two interesting questions: Can the South in fact influence its destiny, given the tremendous economic forces that are shaping its new growth, and, even more fundamentally, is there, in fact, a South still in existence? (There is considerable argument that the South has—to borrow from the title of a recent book by John Egerton—been Americanized).

The answer to the first question is still inconclusive. However, the whole thrust of the Southern Growth Policies Board has been to identify trends in the South, to address them rationally, and to recommend policies that make the Southern states masters, at least to some degree, of their future. The answer to the second question seems to be that the South may indeed have lost much of its distinctiveness, both on its negative and positive characteristics, but, amazingly, "Southerners" may have been affected little if any at all by that loss. One of the most interesting observations developed with Southern youth generally is that they feel very Southern. Their generation has grown up on national TV and McDonald's hamburgers, but they still feel unique as Southerners. Most surprising of all, black students share this same sense.

In the Fall 1972 issue of the *Southern Journal* of the LQC Lamar Society, there was a report of an informal seminar at The University of Alabama on "New Southerners and an Old South." The students who met with me and Dr. McKenzie included the president of the Afro-American Association, John Bivens, who had just returned from a national caucus of black political leaders in Gary, Indiana. John's "Southerness" was as evident there as Robert Toomb's was in the 1860 Democratic convention.

Bivens, speaking with a deep sense of outrage over a new kind of prejudice, said, "I went to the national conference of blacks in Gary, Indiana. I went with the Alabama delegation, and we were not treated as a part of the national entity. No other section of the country was treated with as much disrespect as our section, and yet at the same time we knew that our section was more politically sophisticated than any other section."

His response was equally Southern, "It (the treatment of the black Southerners) didn't insult us at all because we understood that it was not our loss at all. It was their loss."

In sum, the force of Southern self-consciousness seems to me as powerful as it has ever been. The real questions are to what ends that force will be applied, to what new myths will we respond about who we are and where we are destined to go, and with what new blueprints will we try to plan our growth. Out of all the possibilities and options, I am still left with the conviction that our brightest future is going to be some reflection of the best that we can now see about us—and within us.

NOTES

[1]This theme was developed in the 1971 commencement address made to Judson College in Marion, Alabama.

[2]These remarks were made to the 1973 International Insurance Seminar in Madrid, Spain.

[3]Also from the remarks to the 1973 International Insurance Seminar in Madrid, Spain.

[4]From "Another New South," a paper delivered at Kennesaw Junior College in Georgia in 1971.

[5]Also from "Another New South," a paper delivered at Kennesaw Junior College in Georgia in 1971.

[6]From a 1971 address to the Huntsville Chamber of Commerce.

The New South—Again, or The View from Inside the Carpetbag

PETER SCHRAG

PETER SCHRAG—Peter Schrag is a widely published commentator on the American scene and, although he has lived mainly in New York, Massachusetts, and most recently California, he has covered the South on a number of assignments.

Schrag was born in Karlsruhe, Germany, and educated in the New York City public schools and at Amherst College, where he received his A.B. in 1953. He has continued his association with Amherst, serving as assistant secretary of the college and director of publications from 1955 to 1956 and instructor in American Studies, 1960–64.

Since 1966 Schrag's interest in education has taken a slightly different direction. He left the classroom to become associate education editor of the *Saturday Review*, 1966–68, executive editor, 1968–69, and editor at large, 1969–73. From 1969–70 he was an editor at *Change* magazine.

His in-depth investigations into American education and the Boston school system in particular have resulted in a number of articles and reviews in such magazines as *Harper's, The Nation, The New Republic, Atlantic, Commentary, Commonweal,* and *World* among others and in six books: *Voices in the Classroom* (1965), *Village School Downtown* (1967), *Out of Place in America* (1971), *The Decline of the WASP* (1972), *The End of the American Future* (1973), and most recently *Test of Loyalty: Daniel Ellsberg and the Rituals of Secret Government.*

Schrag has been a trustee of the Emma Willard School in Troy, New York, and a member of the Committee on the Study of History. He has been since 1971 a member of the editorial board of *Social Policy* and a member of the editorial board of *Columbia Forum* since 1972.

In 1971–72 Schrag was a Guggenheim Fellow; in 1973–74 he was a Professional Journalism Fellow at Stanford University.

In recent years, Schrag's assignments and journalistic projects have taken him into the South to cover such events as the inauguration of the black Greene County, Alabama, government in January of 1971 and the Charles Evers campaign for governor of Mississippi. In 1971 he wrote, for *Saturday Review*, "New Beat in the Heart of Dixie," an article on The University of Alabama.

I suppose my only legitimate claim to being a commentator on the New South is that I have visited this region four times in the past five years. The first time, I came to do a piece on The University of Alabama. The second time I was planning to attend the inauguration of the Greene County government on January 15, 1971, but I had to return to New York sooner than I had expected. I returned for a couple of weeks in the fall of 1971 to look at Greene County and to cover, among other things, the Charles Evers campaign for governor of Mississippi. My fourth visit was to present the paper on which this essay is based.

The trip in the fall of 1971 was also an attempt to deal with a current, and, I think, partly Northern-inspired idea that there was something special going on in the South, that there was something particularly hopeful about the South, that in fact, as against a country which was despondent—at the end of its imagination about how to deal with its terrible problems—the South offered certain ideas and hopes. That is the reason I went to Greene County, the reason I went and looked at the Evers campaign, and the reason I looked at what was then a very interesting organization called the Gulf Coast Pulpwood Association, which, in the meantime, has had its problems. What fascinates me most about the South, however, has to do with our common need for some kind of mythology, some kind of myth or hope for rejuvenation and for ideas. There is a necessity in this country for a generic west, for some kind of frontier. I am not talking now about a physical frontier necessarily, but some kind of frontier of ideas and of expectations, a kind of generic west in America. On my last trip in '71 I was doing the legwork for a book called the *End of the American Future*. I came down to see whether in fact that whole mythology (which is partly created by Southerners and partly by *Time* and *Newsweek*) really stood for something. At that time the slogan was "Southern Progress without Northern Mistakes." That was the refrain of something that you probably all know called the LQC Lamar Society. The LQC Lamar Society may, in the meanwhile, pardon my ignorance, have gone to its reward, but I doubt it. But even if it has, I am sure that the spirit is still alive. I had a kind of funny time with the LQC Lamar Society because it seemed to me that the LQC Lamar Society was unaware of, or tended to belittle, problems that I felt were serious—more serious than they believed.

But before I get into that, perhaps I can explain a little bit more about that feeling, that vision, by quoting—by doing something that is really quite terrible—which is to quote a little bit of your own stuff. I wrote this after that '71 trip:

Old ghosts kept coming back. Again it was the new South, the new, new South, looking away now from dusty crossroads and the men in the white sheets, looking now to suburbs, electronics plants, country clubs and moderation. Talk progress, talk new attitudes, talk change. New men, new faces, new rhetoric. But the old myth survived, became part of progress itself and each time we tried to destroy or explain it or debunk it we seemed to give it new life. Perhaps the myth of the South was still necessary to our image of America, was something we needed to establish connections with the tragedy and darkness that shape the experience of other men in other places. Through the South, through some Faulknerian reconstruction, perhaps, we might join the rest of humanity, could make common cause with Greeks and Frenchmen and Italians. We spoke about the new South, read the statistics, listened to the rhetoric, said the cliches, mentioned the names of new men: Carter, Scott, Bumpers, Askew, but each time the scent of honeysuckle and reprocessed magnolias returned as strong as ever.

Returned enlarged: by God, maybe the South would save us all, maybe the South contained a real American future. "I would see among blacks a new commitment to Mississippi as a place," wrote Willie Morris in 1970. "Expressions of the love and loyalty to Mississippi as a society worth working for, as a frontier to regaining a lost quality in the American soul." The less romantic among us would say it in other ways, more hard-headed ways, Southern progress without Northern mistakes, growth without pollution, integration with courtesy and understanding, a chance even for a new progressive era in American politics. The South as redeemer. "It may be the South," wrote Marshall Fraley in *Life,* "where the nation's general malaise of racial alienation first finds resolution. Not in the order of division prophesized by the old segregationist/apologists, but in the formal advent of a single people unique and richly dimensioned."

There is obviously a split vision in all that; I knew it then and I know it now. It is something that Paul Gaston talked about in *The New South Creed.* I think it probably is clear enough from this quote:

> The myht of the New South appeared ot be losing its *raison d'etre.* Southerners accepted new racial patterns that gave to the black more dignity and greater opportunity than he had ever known before—only to see sharply highlighted the inadequacies of integration and the immensity of the problems caused by a heritage of oppression. The region's continuing economic progress, more substantial than ever before, was beset by the same kind of critiques that confounded national advances. Its growing identity with the national viewpoint, made possible initially by the nationalization of the race problem, was unrewarded by a sense of relief and achievement because the nation itself appeared to have lost a sense of destiny. Thus deprived of the large frame of reference which had always conditioned its character and given it its special appeal, the myth paradoxically pictured a regional way of life in harmony with a mirage.

I do not think I need to explain that any more except to say that the problem was that there was no model, and that, in a sense, two things were going on at the same time. And those things got confused and mixed and I think, to some extent, they still are. On the one hand there was the South as redeemer, the South as model; and on the other there was the South catching up with the nation. And those were both used as illustrations of the same kind of reconciliation. Or the same kind of progress. But there is another problem, again a problem partly created by Northerners, and that is that we as Northerners or as outsiders are asking too much. I think some of us were demanding of the South something that we

had a hard time doing ourselves; we have discovered in the last
ten years, particularly in the last five years, how hard it is. We
started prematurely by celebrating something that was not really
there, and when we discovered that it was not there we cursed
the South for having failed our expectations. I saw it quite plainly
in the Evers campaign in 1971. There was a tendency toward
premature celebration among Evers' campaign workers. They
celebrated by saying, "Look, here is this man who is able to
campaign all over Mississippi and nobody is shooting at him. He
can walk into all these old towns where people used to be lynched,
and he can stand up on the Court House steps and the Sheriff
makes a ritual of protecting him instead of arresting him." They
were talking seriously, about how he might have a chance to win.
And Evers, who was a kind of fascinating character, went around
saying, "Sure, we'll win big." I think most people knew he was
not going to win, but they were hoping that his campaign would
at least help get a lot of other black candidates—local candidates—
into office. Well, it turned into a disaster. Nearly all of them lost.
The outsiders said that the election was stolen, which, in some
places, it was. But I think the more important thing was that they
then began again to say, "Nothing's changed. It's the same old
thing," without understanding that two things had somehow
triumphed simultaneously and had lost out simultaneously. The
Old South had reasserted itself, but in more subtle ways, not with
bullets, but at the ballot box. It was kind of a con, it was kind of
a hustle, a Chamber of Commerce trick, but it was also, of course,
proof that at least at some level the style had changed. Since the
"New South" was there in that new style of civility and tolerance,
of superficial tolerance, there was evidence for the news magazine
kind of celebration. At the same time, at least in the back counties,
it made very little difference. No black candidate was lynched that
I know of, but very few were elected, and fewer still, once elected,
have any real power.

Another thing that people outside have not fully appreciated is
that in addition to all the issues that are always talked about in
connection with the South—absentee ownership, poverty, the race

issue, and so on—is what I would call the battle with time. It is hooked up with the race issue, but I do not think it is all of it. Obviously this is a country that is youth oriented and that fears maturity, that fears old age, but I think it was more apparent to me in that last trip, particularly in Mississippi, than anything that I have ever seen elsewhere in this country. The kind of thing that people were trying to preserve—and now I am talking about middle-class Mississippians—was a moment in time. I went to a number of political meetings, but the one that really struck me was a political rally in Jackson of middle and upper middle-class Mississippians a few days before the primary. Maybe I do not need to describe people in terms of hairstyles and dress—the bouffant hairdos and the men's white shoes—but the thing that really overwhelmed me was that during the year 1971 the Pride of Mississippi Orchestra was playing nothing but Glenn Miller. And it suddenly struck me—and maybe this is strictly my imagination, maybe it is that myopia from inside the carpetbag—that people were not trying to preserve the year 1850, and they were not trying to preserve magnolias and honeysuckle. What they were trying to preserve was that one short moment, first of all when they were young, and when things seemed beautiful, and secondly, in the unique history of the South, the one moment during and after the Second World War when the South, having been part of that war and having been part of the what seemed to be a kind of reunified country, seemed to be part of America, was beginning to rise in some way and, at the same time, had not yet needed to confront the reality of that reunification, and particularly the Brown decision. It was a kind of lovely moment, the period between 1945 and 1954, when everything seemed to be working but when the hard issues, not only in the South but elsewhere, had not been faced. And I am not sure that, despite all of the talk of the New South, the issue has been faced yet.

I must confess I have made some errors myself in my observations about the South. Like a lot of people who came down here I demanded too much. I imposed too many expectations. I was hard on a number of people whom I took to task. I think

they should have been taken to task, but I do not think I was
sympathetic enough with their problems. One of them was the
president of The University of Alabama, whom I have seen since
and whom I like. But I was hard on him. I thought that people
like him were not taking a sufficient stand on behalf of students,
on behalf of integration, on behalf of a lot of things. I do not
think I quite understood their sense—and maybe they did not
understand it themselves, but they certainly have it—their sense
of how difficult a lot of things are in this country. Back in 1970
David Mathews, in the best Lamar tradition, was talking about
turning this university into a meeting place where the bankers and
the populists could meet and interact, and where the racists and
the integrationists could meet, all of that. And I thought well,
that is a nice cliché for a university. But I am not sure that he
did not understand more than I did about how loaded parts of
this region were with all kinds of explosive things. He understood
some of the subtleties and I did not. I do not think I necessarily
like that. I do not want it to be that way, but I think that is the
way it is. People used to talk about Southern charm, and I finally
began to realize that Southern charm and Southern politics were
all the same thing. And that the charm was partly genuine and
was partly a way of hustling people—it was a con. But it was a
con in an area where certain kinds of candor were pretty dangerous.
And certain kinds of openness, it seems to me, were dangerous.
And I think for an outsider, it is sometimes hard to understand
when the candor is tolerable and when it is not tolerable. The kind
of liberalism that is taken for granted in Cambridge and in Berkeley and in New York—the cocktail party stuff—is for real down
here. If you are going to take that position, or at least at one time
if you were going to take that position, you might well get yourself
shot. It is not for free the way it is in a lot of places where I go
and where I used to live. Now I am sure a lot of that has changed.
But I still know a lot of people who got crosses burned on their
lawns for their troubles. Some of them live on this campus or live
in this town. So I don't think I gave, and I do not think the
North in general gave, enough credit on that issue. It is easier

to say that now than it was five years ago because the North has obviously failed horrendously; as a region we have nothing to brag about—not very much. And so a lot of things have to be reexamined, not by way of saying that racism is okay, but by way of understanding a little more how difficult the problems are, how subtle they are, how easy it is to talk those things away, how easy it is for *Time* magazine or *Newsweek* or Peter Schrag to get conned by the glass and the plastic and the electronics plants and the suburbs, and how easy it is for us to impose our expectations on Southern charm, Southern hospitality, and Southern civility. One of the things that has not yet been fully tested is whether that civility can survive genuine integration. That civility was easy when everybody had his place. Civility is much harder to maintain when you are not sure of places and status.

A lot of the things about the South in which people invested their faith have not come through. We should have known that. Greene County has its problems, and they are serious. Despite the optimism of journalists—recently another piece appeared in a magazine called *Southern Voices*—it is not yet the great monument to, and the great model for, all our hopes. There is still the uneasy coexistence between the old and the new, or, better, between the old and the middle and the new. There is in fact a new South, but it is not the Southeast, it is not the South of mythology, and it is not even the South of the Rising South of the old Confederacy. It is a South characterized by a certain kind of political and economic power that is going to be very significant in this country. If you take a map of the United States—you have to do a little fudging—and you draw a line across that map east-west, from Richmond, Virginia, to San Jose, California, and you divide the country that way, you may have a better simple explanation of current American politics and economics than you can get by using the old clichés: New England—rock-ribbed, Republican, conservative, Yankee; the middle Atlantic States; the old South, the old Confederate Southeast, the Midwest—conservative Republican; the West, and so on. Draw that line and look at that southern tier. Arizona, Southern California, New

Mexico—cheating now with my map—Colorado, Texas, Oklahoma, Arkansas, and then everything to the Atlantic—Atlanta,
Houston, Dallas, Phoenix, Los Angeles, San Diego—have a great
deal in common in terms of the kind of money, first generation
money, new people, political attitudes, votes, and so on. This,
is, as I said, rather simple-minded, and there are all kinds
of exceptions, but it makes sense. This is Nixon country,
from San Clemente to Key Biscayne. It is the country of
defense industry: the proportion of defense contracts, in this
half of the country, is disproportionate to the population. The old
cliché about the Midwest being conservative and Republican
simply does not work anymore. The liberal voices of the
United States Senate, for example, have to a large extent been
Midwesterners. South Dakota, Iowa, Indiana, Illinois, Minnesota, Michigan have been represented by liberals and doves, for
the most part. The conservatives in the Senate—if that is what
they are—have been largely people who come from below that
line, Goldwater, Fannin, Tower, Bentsen, Eastland. Those confrontations over the next few years, those north-south confrontations may get more serious. The country has started to sort itself
out across that line. In part it is the sunshine seekers, in part it is
the kind of industry, and in part it is simply the fact that everything below that line was basically undeveloped or underdeveloped
fifty years ago. This is the developing part of the United States.
Now again there are exceptions. Somebody pointed out to me
that Senator Jackson does not come from the South, and Boeing
is in Seattle. But at the same time, the bulk of the defense interests
are located in the Southern tier, and the oil, and the military. The
officers come from Georgia and Alabama and retire in Dallas and
San Diego. This area of the country is almost totally dependent on
technology; it could not have really developed without technology,
without heavy inputs of water and energy, and without air conditioning. Southern California would become a desert if we did
not ship them water from Northern California. When there is
talk about the South catching up with the country, whatever that
is, it really means that the South is going to catch up with, and

going to become part of, that tier, a tier of newly made men, of newly developed industry, of new fortunes as compared to the old fortunes. People like Carl Oglesby and Kirk Sale have talked about the division between the Yankees and Cowboys; the Yankees are our people and the Cowboys are your people, a first generation of new capitalists, money, and power just establishing themselves. The Yankees are the old power and the old money. The thing that worries me is that in the process of becoming "Americanized" as part of that Southern tier, the South will, like the Southwest, develop a terrible passion for the antiseptic lifestyle of the suburbs, of shopping centers, will abandon whatever there is of civility and personal interaction and concern, and replace them with a style of life that is typified by Los Angeles or San Diego, a kind of rootless, unbased, impersonal style, unconcerned with community, with no sense of interrelationships, a life where the only civic order is the order of the freeway, where everybody lives in his own private universe connected only to the radio station that he listens to in his automobile. The one thing that makes tolerance easy in a place like Los Angeles as compared, say, to a place like New York is the fact that you really, never really, have to rub elbows with anybody. It is very easy to solve the race problem that way; you just put everybody in his own automobile. And unless you try to segregate freeways, which nobody has proposed, there will be no confrontations because there is no personal interaction. And that can pass as tolerance. Perhaps it's easier to put people in cells; then there is no risk that they will hurt each other.

I think that the risk has to be taken—Los Angeles solved the problem in the antiseptic way—because the consequences of that passion for the antiseptic are going to get enormous and extremely dangerous. There is a growing intolerance toward any sort of abnormality, intolerance for any kind of deviance, and intolerance toward once tolerated kinds of craziness. And the technology to enforce that intolerance is spreading. Behavior modification drugs, surveillance, screening, adjustment, data banks, and all of it. That technology is going to grow, and it is going to become more significant. The reason I mention it here, and this again is probably part of my Northern carpetbaggers mythology, is that I still live to some extent with some Faulknerian illusions. In a way, I think, the South has always been able to live with some of those elements of craziness, of odd behavior, has simply lived with them. One of the things that strikes you, for example, about reading Southern literature is that it is full of cripples, of people that are deformed, stunted, and often demented. The rest of the country, in the name of progress, is becoming less and less tolerant of that kind of thing. And I think it is going to institutionalize that intolerance. In all kinds of ways we are going to rationalize our intolerance of deviance by saying we are just trying to take care of all those poor kids who are hyperactive, brain damaged, disabled, freaky by trying to head off delinquency before it occurs, by trying to head off school problems before they occur. We are going to get everybody tested, and then we are going to treat them. There is going to be a lot of pressure to start treating everyone; the reason it has not happened quite as extensively as some people would like is because the technology is still a little crude. They want to do it, but they do not quite know how, unfortunately. Not yet. But one of these days they are going to know how. On issues like privacy and meddling with people's heads those old conservatives from south of that line that I drew are a hell of a lot better than most of my liberal friends from north of that line. At the moment, people like Barry Goldwater and Barry Goldwater, Jr., and Sam Ervin, despite his bad record before Watergate, are at least talking the right way. I am not going to eulogize or to idolize Senator Ervin, but people who have come out of that same kind of conservatism may be more able to resist than anybody else. The South has lived with deviance and craziness—I hope this is not another illusion—and I hope that in the long run the South, in the name of progress, does not get hoodwinked into becoming Los Angeles. That, I think, would be worse than the old South ever was.

One Student's Perspective

JOSEPH B. DOUGHTY, JR.

JOSEPH B. DOUGHTY, JR.—Joseph Doughty, a senior majoring in English and Psychology, was a student enrolled for credit in this symposium, "The Rising South." Doughty came to The University of Alabama in 1970 on a football scholarship after attending high school in his home state of Minnesota. He had, however, spent his summers in Gadsden, Alabama, at the home of his mother's family.

Combining his interests in psychology and photography, Doughty, now a graduate of The University of Alabama, has recently completed a book, *Mirages Upon a Moment,* which will be published by The University of Alabama Press in the near future.

Four years ago, while I was driving through a part of South Alabama, an incident occurred that had little significance for me until I remembered it while participating in "The Rising South" symposium. My changed understanding of this incident exemplifies for me what I gained from the papers presented.

Having traveled several sweltering hours in search of some likely antique dealers, I slowed my car as I saw ahead a small, rather obtrusive roadside drive-in that would, no doubt, have something to quench a thirst. It was not until I approached the gravel clearing upon which sat "Amigo's," that I noticed, not twenty yards my way and on the same side of the road, an old building, rotted and falling down. There was no glass in the windows, and the roof, which had extended out over a porch that still contained nameless, rusty entanglements of wire and metal, had partly collapsed on one side, like a large old eye about to wink shut. A faded, sunbleached sign that still hung to the unwinking side of the roof

117

read: "Sanders Bodine Mercantile and General Farm Supply." Old Mr. Bodine's store was now surrounded by a junkyard. Weeds grew three and four feet high out of the centers of old tires and other refuse. Having stopped the car to take in this scene, which in and of itself was the best "antique" I had seen all day, my thirst reminded me of Amigo's, and I pulled into his gravel drive.

A man in his middle thirties came to the counter window, wiping his hands on a dirty apron. He was unshaven and more than slightly unkempt, and he smiled widely as he pulled aside the screen door on the counter window, revealing a mouth less than full of teeth. He returned a few moments later with the lemonade I had ordered, and I took a seat upon a little bench on the side of the building that afforded a view of the interesting remains just down the road. I wondered about the histories contained in this crust of a building and about who Mr. Bodine had been and what the surrounding countryside had looked like fifty or a hundred years ago.

Just as I finished my lemonade and set my empty cup on the counter, I heard someone call to the man who had waited on me. I had thought he was "Amigo" himself, but the voice addressed him as "Mr. Bodine."

At the time, this occurrence did not hold much significance— at least none that impressed me. I merely recognized the irony contained in what could be inferred of the family history among three or four generations of the Bodines. At the time the irony meant nothing to me with respect to the South or my own South-ernness. "The Rising South," however, did much to bring the significance of the preceding anecdote, and many other things, up from the fringes of my consciousness of the South.

During this symposium we were presented with stimulating, educated, and in some cases eminently educated, viewpoints on widely variant aspects of the South and Southern life. While the paper topics were diverse, they complemented more than con-tradicted each other. For the student who participated in the symposium, "The Rising South" was more an experience than just another college course taken among a collage of academic calisthenics.

Personally, the experience startled what had been an ephemeral sense of "Southernness" that had slept on the edge of my understanding of myself as a Southerner and directed it toward the beginning of a solid consciousness about the South, about being Southern. I realized the impact of the experience the weekend following the symposium. Traveling through the countryside of South Alabama on the way to the Gulf, I suddenly realized that I had been taking every back road I could find and that I was being affected by all that could be taken in. I looked at the land and relished it as I always have, but there was something new, something conscious, something that my experience was bringing to bear on the red clay, the truck patches, and the pine barrens. This conscious awareness gave a deep sense of understanding when I drove over the same road as four years before to find not only that the old eye had winked shut and the building was now a pile of rubble, but also that Amigo's was boarded up, another closed chapter of a Southern family history. It was this same consciousness that saw in a new light an old black man leading a mule down the side of the road, a spreading and lofty mansion sitting agelessly on the quiet mainstreet of a small South Alabama town, a massive industrial park belching forth a billowing cloud over the verdant countryside.

I saw and appreciated these things with a new sense of their significance and connectedness as things uniquely Southern, and as things that bore on my own Southernness—past, present, and future. I thought of change and transition, of paradox and tradition. The sight of the old black man and his mule brought back Tom Gilmore speaking before a group of college students. I thought of George Tindall's explication of the black man's lot before the time of lynching laws, of Tom Gilmore's account of an incident during the civil rights movement when he threw himself over the body of a woman who was being beaten with a riot stick. I thought of freedom marches to Birmingham, Montgomery, and Selma, of George Wallace's stand in the doorway at The

University of Alabama and of his crowning the University's first black homecoming queen. The ante-bellum mansion, elegant and still with towering white Corinthian columns, reminded me of the family histories that had been told and retold to me. I recalled Pat Derian's depiction of the "Southern belle" and Louis Rubin's perspectives on Faulkner, Wolfe, and Caldwell. Watching the gun-metal clouds burst from the stacks of the industrial plants brought back the exhortations of Verda Horne, the hard-line labor presentation of Barney Weeks, the role David Mathews assigned to planning in the future of the South, and Peter Schrag's "carpet-bagger" insights as to what that future ought to be.

These references are to people, but they also represent a conscious sensitization to insights into the South that are beginning to grow. The people mentioned arise out of an experience, and they are metaphors for elements, events, and concepts that collect around what used to be only transient intimations of the South and that which is Southern, but that now particularize the South and Southernness in a manner never before attainable. I for one have become more attuned to and have gained a clearer sense of that which can be identified as intrinsically Southern and of what being Southern means to the individual Southerner.

"The Rising South," a college course, but more importantly, an experience, has indeed given a new significance to living in the South. The mythology and actuality of the Southern past, present, and future that used to float in the ether of day by day un-importance, now stands objectified and demanding attention. The course lends the beginnings of coherence to entities, events, and concepts that have lain dormantly subliminal, but that have always been a part of Southern experience. It identifies and organizes their interplay and discord and brings to recognition the beginning of an understanding of the South as a concept, the subtleties of which each Southerner must comprehend for him—or her—self. I have been brought nearer to this concept and its understanding and nearer to the role the South and its people must play in regard to each other and to their land.

Index